Jean Anderson was born in Glasgow. Having contracted tuberculosis as a child, Jean's education was delayed. Nevertheless, she went on to university, where she qualified as a teacher of English. Her teaching career saw her in schools in both Glasgow and Angus, from where she retired in 1996.

After retirement from mainstream education, Jean continued to work as a private tutor and a freelance journalist. It was during this point in her life that Jean decided to write *Wine Alley Days* – the story of her family's return to Glasgow after wartime evacuation.

Wine Alley Days

Jean Anderson

Wine Alley Days

Olympia Publishers
London

www.olympiapublishers.com
OLYMPIA PAPERBACK EDITION

Copyright © Jean Anderson 2014

The right of Jean Anderson to be identified as author of
this work has been asserted in accordance
with sections 77 and 78 of the Copyright,
Designs and Patents Act 1988.

All Rights Reserved

No reproduction, copy or transmission of this publication
may be made without written permission.
No paragraph of this publication may be reproduced, copied or transmitted save
with the written permission of the publisher, or in accordance
with the provisions
of the Copyright Act 1956 (as amended).

Any person who commits any unauthorised act in relation to
this publication may be liable to criminal
prosecution and civil claims for damage.

A CIP catalogue record for this title is
available from the British Library.

ISBN: 978-1-84897-404-3

(Olympia Publishers is part of Ashwell Publishing Ltd)

This is a work of fiction.
Names, characters, places and incidents originate
from the writer's imagination. Any resemblance to actual
persons, living or dead, is purely coincidental.

First Published in 2014

Olympia Publishers
60 Cannon Street
London
EC4N 6NP

Printed in Great Britain

To Neil: the man who would not give up,
and to my brave, crazy family

Acknowledgement

To all, family and friends who listened to me and encouraged my writing ambitions. Particularly to my late father, who started me off when he visited me in hospital.

PROLOGUE

Family gatherings are probably the same for all families. Everybody contributes to the nostalgia. There is a collective version of all the major events which have become part of the family history. Everybody laughs, or is indignant as they remind each other of what they have gone through as a family. Sometimes they are sad, but only briefly, as they recall those who are absent.

My family – the Wallaces – are no different. Whether the occasion is a funeral, wedding, Hogmanay or just a get together, the ritual is the same: The four eldest go over stories that have become legend, about the time we spent living in the country as evacuees sent there from Glasgow to keep us safe from the bombing. I remember some of them, or I think I do because I have heard them so often. The themes are about how we were 'sent from pillar to post' because nobody wanted to put up a woman and six weans; how the locals called us 'Glesca keelies' and the school teachers despised us, because we were smart at our school work. Most of the stories are funny and show us always coming out on top, and emphasise our closeness as a family.

It's the stories about our life after the war, when we returned to our home city of Glasgow, that are a constant source of wonder to me. Our ages range from seven months (wee John, born nine months after Johnnie, our dad, returned from the war); Billy, six; me, Maggie, eight, Roddy, ten; Conn, twelve; Nancy, fourteen; and Vicky, the eldest at sixteen – yet we all tell the same versions of the 'big' stories of that time.

I know I remember things differently from the accepted reminiscences, and I would like to know from each of them, how they saw their experiences of living in Wine Alley.

The following narrative is how I imagine them telling their own stories not how the rest of the family want them to be remembered. There are some things in most of the stories that, as a family we seem to have censored, so as not to spoil the hard won solidarity that we have achieved.

CHAPTER ONE

Coming home

"I'll let ye off here son," the driver of the rickety wee bus yelled, over his shoulder to Johnny. "Your wife and weans live in the third house down in main street. It's the misses Mc Whirters' cottage. No, very big for a big family, but a fine wee house. You'll likely get something bigger now that your back, eh?"

"Thanks Jock, I'll find it," Johnnie answered as he jumped off, flicking his fag end to the roadside – there was no pavement – and standing on it.

"Good luck son. I'll probably be seeing you a lot on ma bus." The 'son' had been getting on Johnny's nerves and he was glad to get off the bus before he would have to say something to the old fool.

He lifted his kitbag, slung it on his shoulder and began walking down the main street, of the small Ayrshire village, where he would be reunited with the wife and weans he had not seen for five years. All over Britain, men were going through the same experience – some found it at least as frightening as facing the enemy had been.

Johnnie was a day later than he had said in his letter to May. A crowd of ex POWs like himself met up in Glasgow and drunk everything they could get their hands on. They had dreamt of home for five years, yet they had put it off for one more night with their mates. Like putting off that first drink of water after suffering thirst for a long time.

He had taken only a few steps, when he heard the click of high heels behind him, (that had been one of those sounds, that the men had voted, one night was in the top three of those they missed most in the prison camp). A hand grabbed his arm and he turned to face a plump blonde woman, who was laughing and talking at the same time: "You must be Johnny Wallace." She didn't give him a chance to answer. "Come oan, I'll deliver ye to them." She pulled his arm through hers and he knew that the pressure of her round warm breast against his hand was not an accident. He felt that women had all gone 'man daft' since the war, but he did not complain, as she hurried him along the street, stopping at the end of one of a terrace of ancient cottages, with the white wash, badly needing renewed, she pushing him in front of her when May opened the door to her demanding knock.

"Here's your man May," she laughed proudly. "I found him wandering the streets looking for his wife and weans. Come on you lot, I've bought you yer daddy." She hurried out the door, yelling, "I'll see you later May – and you Johnnie."

The first thing May noticed, of the changes in him, was that he no longer had his lovely rory red hair. He still had the thick hair, growing low on his forehead, but now it was the same khaki colour of his army uniform. The second thing was how thin and pale he was. She felt panic, that she didn't know him, and stood still surrounded by six equally still children.

It was not how he had imagined it: None of his children rushed to him with open arms, or said, "Welcome home, Daddy." He had to speak first. He held out his arms to them and said, "Come on then, you'll have to tell me your names," and then turning to Vicky and Nancy, "I think I know who these lovely big girls are – you are my Vicky and Nancy. Are you not going to give your wee daddy a big hug – come on then?"

Nancy moved first, with her hair as red as his had been, all over the place, as usual. She ran into his arms and said, "Welcome home, we thought you were coming yesterday, Mammy baked a cake."

Vicky was next and moved much more slowly, with dignity beyond her years. She was still as beautiful as he remembered. Her hair was darkest brown and combed neatly in a middle parting, with ribbons holding it back from her face, which was serious and a bit impatient at the showing off of her younger sister. It was a beautiful face, with large dark blue eyes, a full-lipped mouth and perfect white teeth. The one feature, which she hated was her turned up nose, about which her brothers had long ago learnt not tease her. She allowed him to give her a hug.

His two eldest sons, whom he only vaguely remembered were next. "I'm Conn," the taller of the two said. He had black hair, like his mother's, and sharp features, which gave him a worried look. He was blushing, and moved back as soon as he introduced himself.

"I'm Roddy," was next – another redhead, with a cocky manner that reminded Johnnie of himself. "I'm the clever one." This thawed them out and they all laughed and teased him about being 'big-headed', which did not faze him a bit.

Then came a little girl, with fair hair and blue eyes, who reminded him of his own sister, long dead. She leaped into his arms and hugged him with her legs. "I'm Maggie, the second youngest. I'm top of the class. Did you get all of my letters I sent you? I'm seven and my birthday's in June." Where the others had moved back beside their mother after their welcomes, she stood beside him, holding on to his leg and talking non-stop, until May told her, "For goodness sake be quiet and let your daddy sit down."

He gently put the wee girl aside and moved towards her. "Do I not get a welcome home from my wife?" he asked, putting his hands on her shoulders. She gave a little a little sound between a sob and a laugh. "Oh Johnnie," she said. "It's good tae see you at last." They kissed as their family stood in a circle around them as if they were watching some sort of ritual. Vicky was the first to break the circle, she went into the scullery and they could hear the sound of the kettle being filled.

"Sit down Johnnie and I'll get your tea. I've managed to scrounge the stuff to bake a cake and I've had to stand guard on it since it came out of the oven." As she turned to follow Vicky he noticed a little figure who had been hiding behind her apron all the time.

"Who's this wee man?" he asked, suddenly realising that only five weans had greeted him.

"It's our Billy," Maggie said. "He's shy."

It wasn't shyness Johnnie saw in his youngest son's eyes: it was resentment, bordering on hatred. He ruffled the boys red curly hair and said, "Hello Billy," and decided to think about getting to the bottom of the bad feelings later on. First he wanted to be with May and be husband and wife again – the weans could wait.

After they had eaten, he put his kitbag down on the floor and opened it. He took out a pile of cigarettes and put them on the table at his side; some silk stockings (from the Yanks) for May and more chocolate bars than they had ever seen in their lives. He had been saving his chocolate ration for them and the expressions of delight on their wee faces – even Billy's – showed him that he'd 'won a watch'.

They crowded round and he gave each of them a whole bar, but said, "Don't eat it all at once, let your tea go down," and turning to Vicky and Nancy "Now are you two big girls goin' to keep an eye on your brothers and sisters while I take yer mammy out for a wee while? Is there a hotel or a pub in the village?"

"We'll watch them," Nancy said. "Can we stay up a bit later and play cards for a while?"

"There's the Boar's Head Hotel and the Queen's," said Vicky. "The Boar's Head is the poshest."

"Snob!" the others said together.

"Maybe we'll go to the two of them then, go get ready hen."

Nancy said May looked like Merle Oberon and Johnnie like James Cagney as they stood at the door waving them off. As the others set up the card table; Maggie lined up her rag dolls to play schools; Billy got out his drawing things; Nancy went through to the scullery. "Back in a mo," she said with a sly look.

They did not have long to wait to find out what she had been up to. The door was thrown open and she stood there flourishing a cigarette, from which she took a deep draw as their mouths hung open in amazement.

"Would anyone like a puff?" she said in her best posh voice.

They all took a turn: Roddy as if he'd been smoking all of his ten years; Vicky coughing until she was blue in the face and Conn until he turned green and dashed for the scullery. Despite the coughing and the sickness they all had a good time that night, and all agreed that it was going to be great having their daddy home – apart from Billy, who just went on drawing.

They were all in bed when May and Johnnie returned. They could hear May singing as they came in the door: "Coming home my darling, coming home to me," and Nancy said she felt happier than she had ever felt in her life, although she felt a bit like crying too. Vicky told her she was soppy, but she felt the same although she would never admit it.

There were only two bedrooms in the cottage – one upstairs, where Roddy and Conn slept in one bed and Nancy and Vicky in the other. Maggie and Billy slept downstairs in a big double bed with May. In their innocence the girls had put their younger brother and sister to bed in the usual place, they had not given a thought to where Johnnie would sleep.

Nancy was sound asleep and Vicky just dropping off, when the bed covers were turned back and Maggie was put gently in beside them. She seemed to be sleeping soundly, then everyone was woken up by the sound of Billy crying and shouting.

"I want tae sleep in ma own bed! A always sleep in there! It's no your bed! Let me down!" and Johnnie came into the room carrying a struggling bundle of rage.

The poor wee boy could not understand why he was being put out of his bed by this strange man and if he had hated him before his usurpation from May's side solidified the feeling for a long time to come. On top of this, his big brothers liked to torment him and made sure he had as little sleeping room as possible; the blankets were pulled off him regularly and they passed wind as near to his face as they could. May worried about him for a while that night, but he was pushed from her thoughts by her fear of what it was going to be like having sex with her man after all these years. She had never really openly and wholeheartedly enjoyed what they did together to make their weans. Decent women put up with it. The man needed to be pleased. It was part of being a married woman. Mind, she had missed the closeness and the kissing, but for the rest she could survive without it. He had told her, as they sat in the hotel bar, that he couldn't wait to get her home. "We've five years to make up for," he said, "and I'm going tae make you glad I'm back." She giggled and clenched her hands to stop them from shaking. She was embarrassed at how much she wanted to be in bed with him. It wisnae decent, she thought.

"A don't think we want mair weans just now," she said. "We're overcrowded as it is."

"If it happens, it happens hen," he said. "There's nothing nicer than a new wee wean."

It did happen.

The first six had been conceived through her submission to his 'rights' as her man. She had enjoyed the closeness and the strength of his manliness, but wondered what all the fuss was about. This conception was different and at last, she understood what sex could be between two people.

He insisted on keeping the light on – it was an oil lamp. The cottage did not have electricity – and undressed her slowly, laughing gently at the long knickers and the suspender belt she wore, while kissing every bit of her, so that she blushed and cried out "Oh don't!", yet not wanting him to stop. It was the first time she had really let herself be taken by the tide of physical pleasure, and each of the four times they did it that night, was better than the last. She blushed at the thought of the weans hearing them and at her shamelessness, but she was taken over by feelings she had not known were hers to enjoy and the tide could not be stemmed, until they fell asleep exhausted. She did not hear him getting up, the first she knew was when a little hand on her shoulder woke her and Maggie laughed. "We've brought you breakfast in bed Mammy, Billy and me helped make it." She smelt the bacon – she never did find out how he had got round the rationing and sat up, pulling the rough blankets up to her neck to cover up her nakedness. Billy stood at the end of the bed and glowered while she ate, the marks of the previous night's tears still on his cheeks. He managed to smile when she patted the bed next o her and said, "Come on and sit here Billy, like a good boy."

The day of Johnnie's coming-home was the start of the happiest times in all of their lives – apart from Billy's who could not get used to being usurped by this strange man, everybody else seemed to love.

He was regarded as a hero in the village, particularly in the two pubs, where he could always persuade the owners to part with a share of their precious store of whiskey for himself and his new cronies. The local boys loved him because he organised a football team and trained with them in the park. Most of the women, young, middle-aged and old loved him and envied May for having such a 'smashin' man.

It was like a long holiday that only Johnnie and May knew could not last forever.

The arrival of wee john, nine months after the homecoming and a letter from the misses McWhirter, made them realise that it was time to go home to where they belonged.

A temporary, partial solution was found to the overcrowding, by Vicky and Nancy going to Glasgow to live with their Granny Ross (Mary's mother) who got them jobs in the fur trade, but Conn and Roddy, Maggie and Billy still had to share one with two beds. He knew that they would have to get a bigger house, where they could all be together with more living space and an inside lavatory and electricity. Although they had been happy there, it was like a camping holiday, with everyone living on top of one another. The letter from the McWhirter sisters was what he needed to make him come out of the dream he had been in since his arrival in the village. He needed to get work and make a life for May and the family.

So he left for Glasgow – to see about a house for a returning hero!

We stood silently in the phone box, Mammy and me staring out at the rain. Nothing was visible beyond the red-rimmed squares of glass and I thought I felt the box move with the wind. The baby stirred inside the plaid, wrapped tightly around Mammy's delicate body, but he slept on. I sneaked a look at her now and then. Her black hair was painted against her high forehead, like rivulets of ink, despite the scarf covering her head (we got soaked on the way to the phone) and her high cheekbones shone red against the paleness of her skin. I always thought she was beautiful, but she would have scoffed at me if I had ever dared to say so. We did not pay compliments to one another in our family. When the phone rang it made us both jump and the baby's eyes flew open, like those of a 'sleeping – doll'.

"Lift it," she said, "and hold it for me. Hello, John!" she shouted. "Is that you? Right. OK. What happened? Did you get it?" I think he told her to calm down, for she took a deep breath and signalled to me, to hold the receiver closer to her ear.

"Oh, that's great," she sighed. "A four apartment? The weans'll not know what tae dae wi' theirsels. Oh that really is marvellous John." I gaped in shock: I had never heard her use the word 'marvellous' before.

"OK, John, I'll see you when you get back tomorra. You can tell me all about it then – cheerio." She nodded to me to put the receiver back and as we pushed together to open the heavy door of the telephone box, I was sure there was a tear mingling with the rain on her cheek.

"You're Daddy's got us a house." She repeated the words she had said to me as we hurried back from the phone – this time to Conn and Roddy, who had the table set for our tea and the potatoes boiling on the erratic range; and Billy, who was playing one of his secret complex games, involving boot – brushes and clothes pegs. My two big brothers had jumped on the misses McWhirter's furniture yelling like banshees. Billy just sat and smiled. As usual I asked the question that mattered to me:

"Where is it? How big is it? Does it have an inside lavvy? Will I have a room tae masel?"

"I don't know much about it yet. You're daddy's goin' to see it the day. He'll stay the night with ye granny, and see your sisters, then come back tomorra. But he says whatever Its like, we'll take it until we get something better. We have to get outta here. The McWhirters want their house back. We're not classed as evacuees any longer – just homeless people, and It's up to Glasgow to give us a house. That's our home town. "It's terrific," Roddy said. " Just thinks, we'll be able to go tae the fitba every Saturday, a' the big Rangers game – come on the Gers!"

"And the pictures," I put in, suddenly seeing a glamorous new life opening up for us. The 'new house' suddenly appeared on my internal sketch pad, where all my dreams were drawn. It resembled Thornfield from 'Jane Eyre' which I was struggling through, but loving with touches of 'The Little House on The Prairie'. How was I to know that such a house would be severely out of place in Govan. It was nothing like the house of my imagination, but in its own way it was paradise to us.

The morning we left Daddy had us all up and 'standing by our beds' by seven o'clock, giving us three hours to make the one hour journey to Girvan, from where we were to get the train to Glasgow at ten o'clock. We were all given a roll, spread thickly with margarine and jam and a cup of tea and told to keep ourselves clean until our transport to the station arrived: This was to be an army lorry, which he had somehow got one of his mates to borrow from a nearby camp. The thought of travelling in such a style was almost better than our excitement at going on the train.

I wish the smell and the noise of that railway station could have been bottled up and 'laid down' like some fine wine. Fairgrounds and smoky fires sometimes bring it back to me, but I wish I could recreate it at will when I feel down, and need a happy memory to lift me up again.

We sat in two rows in the train compartment. It seemed the height of poshness to me, even the jaggy covering on the seats which tickled my legs and made me squirm until Daddy told me to, "Sit still or you'll stand."

Mammy sat at one window seat with the new baby on her lap, wrapped in a tartan shawl and daddy sat opposite, smoking and reading his paper as if he was not with us; Billy sat very close to his Mammy – he was still heartbroken at the arrival of Daddy and then the new baby; I sat between Daddy and Conn, who faced Roddy. We almost filled the compartment apart from two seats that were taken up by an elderly couple, who glowered disapprovingly at us weans for most of the journey and broke the world record for 'tutting' when Mammy sleekitly gave the baby her breast, under the cover of the shawl.

We were all dealing with our excitement in different ways. I watched everything outside and inside the compartment, occasionally looking at myself in the window. I was wearing a blue print dress and a red fluffy cardigan (cast-offs from a neighbour) and I thought I looked a bit like Margaret O'Brien – child film star – with fair hair, instead of black and blue eyes instead of brown. I kept my mouth closed in an enigmatic smile, to avoid showing the gaps in my front teeth; Billy was tying knots in wee John's shawl. I wanted to talk to him about the sights along the route, but he had taken himself into his own wee world, where he always went when he was unhappy – sometimes even when he wasn't.

Conn was making out that he was reading the 'Wizard' but I knew he hadn't once turned the page. He looked white and scared. I thought maybe he didn't like the train. He was never usually scared of anything – even mice. He was wearing a checked lumber jacket that Daddy had bought him and I thought he looked really handsome, with his nearly black hair and thin white face, like the picture of a famous poet in my reading book; Roddy, as usual was acting old – as if he had been on the train hundreds of times and it was nothing to him. I caught him trying to 'stare out' the crabbit old woman who had 'tutted', until her eyes began to water and she got up and went out into the corridor – shaking her head like an angry hen. He was wearing the lumber jacket that Daddy had bought him too and I could see he had stolen some of Daddy's brilliantine to flatten and try to darken his orange hair, which he hated.

Mammy had a wee, square worried frown on her forehead and she was wearing lipstick and powder, with her hair in two kinds of question marks, on her cheeks She spoke quietly to Billy, when he woke up and glared around him: "No' long now son. You'll be seeing your new house." She never spoke to me like that, but I didn't care, I didn't want to be treated like a baby, I was nearly eight, for goodness sake!

Anyway, Daddy winked at me over his newspaper when nobody was looking and made me feel that he and I knew something the rest didn't.

*

The Glasgow subway struck us dumb with fear at first. Daddy carried Billy down the stairs and I almost pulled Mammy's skirt off, clinging to it like a kitten to its mother, while the boys had to take the two suitcases – everything else we owned (not much) had been sent on ahead – which were as big as themselves. Other passengers, quickly took us over, helped to stow the cases and settled us on the train. None of us spoke during the short journey.

Christopher Columbus could not have been more impressed with America, than we were with Govan. Billy was convinced that we had become small, like elves, to get on the subway, and turn to our normal size when we came above ground. None of us laughed at this strange belief. We were too wide-eyed at the sight of the broad streets, lined with tenements. The tallest building the younger members of the family had seen until then had been the village church, but people lived in these three and four storey buildings – we were going to live in one – which were more marvellous and menacing to us than the skyscrapers we had seen in an American picture.

There was a group of men standing at one of the street corners we passed. One of them said: "Well Johnnie Wallace! Nice tae see you," as we walked by, making us feel important that our Daddy was recognised by these tough-looking characters.

At last we turned into the street where we were going to live. It was a potential paradise for playing. There were front gardens, where a few brave blades of grass were trying to break through hard-packed grey soil, edged around by two foot high concrete walls (we learned later that the marks like black blots on their surface, were all that remained of the metal railings that had been removed for the war effort.), which made your feet itch to walk along them and jump from one side of the close mouth to the other. We had never seen closes before.

It was Roddy who first became aware of the man shouting and running behind us. He was waving something pointed and shiny in his hand.

"Daddy, that man is chasing us!" he called out and began to run, with the huge suitcase battering against his legs.

"Just get behind me," Daddy said, shoving Mammy with the baby, roughly behind him, putting himself between the man and his family. "I'll sort this out. What's your game Mack? Do ye want something frae me?" Then they saw the kitchen knife in his hand and screamed out in terror and excitement as Daddy reached out and grabbed his wrist.

"For Chrissake, John." He winced in pain, trying to free his wrists. "A was only bringing this tae ye. It fell outta the case the lad's carryin'. A didnae mean tae frighten yer wife an' weans." Daddy let go his wrist and laughed as he shook the fellow's hand. "Thanks wee son," he said. "I've been away too long. I'll see you in the pub some night – buy ye a hauf, ch?

That was the first of many laughs we got in the Wine Alley. Conn must have left a trail of cutlery from the subway station, because there was hardly any left, when the case was unpacked and we had to share three forks and two knifes between us until Mammy got more from Granny Ross: not everyone was as honest as the 'running man' as we referred to him in our family legends.

Living up a close was like in a commune. Everybody know one another's business. It had been a bit like that in the village, but not just as intimate in detail. For example; what was being cooked at every meal; how many baths the family took a week, and at what time; who slept in which bedrooms and what family rows were about, were all in the public domain of close life and were spread to a wider audience via close-mouth gossip sessions, which Mammy was not allowed to join in, by Daddy's decree.

Several of the neighbours – the wives – were leaning out of their windows as we arrived (we soon learned to refer to this custom in true Glasgow fashion as 'hingin oot the windae'). They stared, silently at us as we entered the close, being led by Daddy to the house, on the right of the first landing which already had a brass plate on the door with black letters:' J.WALLACE'.

It was a proud day for us: taking possession of our first real home. Wine Alley was going to be paradise.

*

Green fields, woods and open spaces – the accepted idea of a childhood paradise – could not compete with this: A long lobby, with rooms leading off it; the bathroom and kitchenette at the right hand side; the three bedrooms at the left and the living room facing the outside door at the far end. And, what a view from that living room a railway goods yard, with trains clanking and shunting up and down all day and most of the night! We divided our time between looking out of the window and standing in line to use the flush toilet and run the water.

Keep your woods and fields – this really seemed like paradise to us.

Conn and Roddy appreciated the toilet more than anyone. It had been their job for the years we had spent in McWhirter's cottage, to haul buckets of shit out of the dry lavvy, at the bottom of the garden, once a week and bury the stinking mess in a hole behind the gooseberry bushes (what gooseberries we used to get there! I've never seen bigger or tasted sweeter)

The kitchenette was cramped. We could not all get in at the one time, but it had all the necessities that planners had decided 'homeless' people should be grateful for: a double sink, one deeper than the other, for washing clothes in; a metal clothes boiler; a cooker; some shelves; one food cupboard and a coal bunker, of all things. It was better than having to cook meals in an old kitchen range and it did not matter about the poor shelf and cupboard space as we had little to fill them with.

Daddy left Mammy to it and went off for a pint. He felt that he had done more than was called for, by sticking with them this long and the weans were getting on his nerves running from room to room as if they were at the 'shows'. By that time Nancy and Vicky were there to help with the baby and making the tea so he would 'just be in the road' man's universal cop out!

Billy and I were cycling up and down on his tricycle; Conn and Roddy assembling the iron bedstead in the room they had claimed as theirs; Wee Jay (the name the baby was called now) was screaming and Mammy was trying to referee a row between Nancy and Vicky about who should peel the potatoes when the door was thrown open and the hall shook as if an elephant had entered the lobby.

"Dae ye realise there are folk livin' under ye?" This was our downstairs neighbour's way of introducing herself: Maisie Ranachan, the fattest woman any of us had ever seen. She had a round face, made rounder by the fact that her hair was pulled close to her skull by a hairnet; black glinty eyes; breasts reaching somewhere around her great thighs and legs like an elephant in ballet tights. She wore a flowery wraparound overall, which made her look like a burst parcel.

"You're shakin' every light in ma hoose. You'll have tae keep yer weans under control – so ye will."

Mammy gave the nearest wean to her a slap on the ear – it happened to be Roddy – and said, "Sorry, they'll be quiet in future. They're not used to living in a close." For some reason she was speaking posh, and between this and the appearance of the amazing 'fat lady' we were in danger of mass-hysteria, by the time she banged the door as she was leaving.

So this was our new home – Wine Alley Days had begun.

May in the park

CHAPTER TWO

Mistakes

MAY'S STORY

The old sour-face sitting opposite us on the train looked as if she had the dry boak when I slipped my nipple into the wean's mouth (I kept my shawl round me, but she knew what I was doing) I had been going to go to the toilet to feed him, but John said these places were filthy and it was a perfectly natural thing to do – if anybody objected they could object to him. There wasn't many people had the nerve to do that, even when I first met him. He had the reputation 'you don't want to fall out wi' John Wallace' people used to say and it was even more definite now. Since he had come back from Germany, there was a look in his eye like a dog gets when it's guarding a bone or a cat when she is protecting her litter. I wish I could take him to meet all the officials and do-gooders that had pushed us around (treating me like a daft wee lassie instead of a married woman wi' six of a family) While he was a prisoner of war and we had been evacuees. He would have shrivelled their petty, hard wee hearts with a look.

Anyway it didn't matter now. He had forced the Corporation to re-house us, back in Govan where we belonged. They had made the excuse that we didn't count as a priority as we hadn't had a house of our own before the war and people who had been bombed out of their homes came first.

I don't know how he did it but John made the man in the housing office change his mind and offer us a four apartment in Kellas street – not a very nice area – but all that I could think about was – at last after living in lodgings, broken down farm labourer's cottages and never having enough room we were going to have a home of our own with a kitchen and an inside toilet. I wouldn't have changed it for Balmoral.

It wouldn't just be a new house; it would be the start of the new life, John had talked about in his letters from the POW camp (Funny wee letters on thin paper, with black blobs on them sometimes where they had been censored by the War Office).

The first few months he had been back had been perfect. He was a hero in the village where we stayed and there were victory celebrations and getting to know the weans after five years away, and wee Jay on the way after he was just back a month so that people winked and made suggestive remarks about us 'not wasting any time' but nothing bad – as if they were all involved in us being back together.

But then he started to get restless; he was nearly always half-cut or really drunk and he had begun to criticise everything I did with the weans: I hadn't fed them properly; they were all too skinny; the boys were sissies and the girls jobs were shameful. I had done nothing right for his family while he was helpless and relying on me. There was no point in trying to explain what it had been like trying to look after six weans without a man at your back and not knowing whether you have your man back alive. He just said, "Thousands of women coped." I had been too easy-peasy about everything according to him.

For the first time since we married, we had furniture that belonged to us, in our new house. It was noisy and chaotic – everybody arguing about what they would have and the weans playing on a trike in the lobby as if it was a race track: until the woman downstairs came up to complain.

She just barged right in and shouted at me in front of the weans (John had gone out for a pint just after we arrived) and as usual I didn't know how to stand up for myself. I always felt like a daft wee lassie next to the other wives and mothers, as if they were real and I was just playing at it. How was I going to keep six weans from making a noise? They didn't even know when they were making a noise and her remarks about washing the stairs and using the drying green made me wish we were still evacuated.

John made it all right when he came in, loaded down with fish suppers and sweeties for the weans – he'd even bought me a wee miniature of sweet sherry. As soon as the dishes were done we were all sitting round the fire having a sing song. Nancy and Vicky sung 'Sentimental Journey' copying the Andrews sisters; Conn sung 'When I grow too old to dream' his Granny's favourite; Roddy, Maggie and Billy were too shy to sing alone, but they joined in with me when I sung the songs I had sung to them, as we lay listening to the German bombers going over to bomb Clydebank, when we had been safely in bed in the country. I sung everything they asked for: 'The White Cliffs of Dover'; Bonnie Scotland ; Mary of Argyl and even, just for a laugh, 'Run Rabbit, Run Rabbit', which made Mrs Ranachan bang on the ceiling – crabbit old bitch! John sung 'Dixie' (his own version) and 'There ain't no Boys Around The Corner' We finished up with 'It's a Long Way to Tipperary' as the weans danced in a Conga off to bed, leaving John and I by the fire as it died down.

"I think we're going to have a good life, May," he said and I felt sure he was right.

He hated the job in the gasworks that the burro had sent him to, but he made jokes about it, saying when he went on the tramcar everyone else got off because of the smell of him. That was the bit that most annoyed him; it made him feel dirty, whereas he was the opposite, always making me keep the fire backed up to the heat the water for baths for him and the weans. Still he said he would stick it out until something better turned up.

The weans were beginning to lose their shyness of him a wee bit, although I warned them not to annoy him when he came in from work and wanted peace to read his paper. He taught the boys to play a game called 'battleships' that kept them quiet for hours, and he gave them all – apart from Nancy and Vicky – haircuts. He said he had cut the other prisoners' hairs in the camp. I could see Conn and Roddy wanted him to talk about when he had been a prisoner and I wished he would tell us what it had been like but he never did – except that one thing he told me. The thing that smashed our new life to dust.

*

Nancy and Vicky were taking it in turns to draw black lines up the back of each other's legs to look like stocking seams, trying not to giggle and have to start all over again as they had done already – twice, when he had said to them, "I hope you two are not planning anything for tomorrow night."

Nancy shook her head and said, "Just Barrowland," and Vicky said:

"I was thinking of going out with a girl from work to see that new Fred Astaire picture – why?" "Because I want you to stay in and keep an eye on things. I'm taking your Mother up the town. She needs a night out after a' the hard work of moving in here wi' you lot and a new wean."

It was the first I heard of it, and I felt my face go scarlet. Before I could start making up excuses not to go – although I was dying to – he said to Maggie, "Go and bring that parcel I left in the kitchen, hen."

It was a blouse! Pale bluey-grey, with pearly buttons from the wee Mandarin collar right down the front, and on the cuffs and sleeves. It was the nicest thing I had ever had to wear, and wrapped in the same parcel, was a pair of fine nylon stockings, the colour of rich tea biscuits. I felt like throwing myself at him; crying; laughing, but instead I said, "I haven't got a decent skirt to wear and what about my hair. You should have given me more warning." It wasn't the first time I had seen that look of disappointment on his face. It happened every time he gave me anything. I don't know why I had to be like that and throw things back at him.

"My dark skirt will go great with it," Nancy said, "and Vicky and I can do your hair."

"You can wear my wee red jigger jacket as well and these black shoes I got last week," Vicky said.

The Saturday night came and I felt like the wee seventeen-year-old lassie that John Wallace had first taken out for a walk along the banks of Clyde.

I couldn't believe he wanted to go out with me. He could have any lassie; in fact the rumour was that he was winching a school teacher and I was just serving in a baker's shop. A lifetime had passed since then and he wasn't taking me for a walk this time.

"A slap-up dinner, a few drinks and the show at the Metropole," he told the girls when they asked where he was taking me – yet I still felt lucky to have been picked by him over all the girls he could have had. I still didn't know what he could have seen in me, but he still made me feel like a wean going on a

Sunday school treat. The dinner was great – he did all the ordering and the waiters hung around him as if he was a real big shot. He had a knack of giving that impression and people treated him accordingly.

We talked more than I ever remember us talking before. He told me how he had loved getting my letters – how they had helped him get through the bad times in the POW camp – and the letters I had got the weans to send him, telling all about themselves. He said it made him feel just a wee bit that he was taking part in their upbringing, although he knew I had the hardest part. He said, some men had stopped getting letters from home after a while and some had even got 'Dear John' letters. I could hardly swallow my food when he told me about that. Then he said, "It's really hard for men, to be away from their wives, you know May," (I can remember it word for word) "and sometimes things happen that they don't mean to happen. I want us to start our new life, with everything between us in the open. I thought of not telling you this, but I think it would be sleekit and lousy, knowing the hard time you've had on your own…"

I shook my head, not wanting him to go on, but he stretched across and took my hand:

"I went wi' a German lassie – just a couple of times: she was lonely and I was lonely. She was the farmer's daughter where we worked. She wasnae a bad lassie; her man was away – missing presumed dead. It just happened. It didnae mean I thought any less of you and the weans. Can you understand, May? I had to tell you. But I want to put it behind us and forget it ever happened, is that OK hen?"

*

I had to put it out of my mind, now his words brought it all back – that one worry that had spoiled his first night home – now I could get rid of it:

Every bit of my skin turned hot and prickly as if it was crackling with heat and I had to take a big gulp of my sherry to wet my throat before I could speak:

"I'm glad you told me," I said (How could I know that I was just about to throw everything away) "Something happened to me, I couldn't write it in a letter to you – the War Office would have censored it out anyway – I didn't know how you would take it. But now that you've told me about the German girl. I know you'll understand how it could happen. It's got nothing to do with what's between us. It doesn't matter at all – as long as we're honest to each other." His face had gone all white and I noticed – too late to shut up – the mad look he got in his eyes, when he had had too much whiskey. But it wasn't that, he had only had two.

"Talk sense!" he said. "What are you havering on about – 'something happened to you'? What do you mean?"

"Like you and the German girl," I whispered "He was a Polish prisoner. He followed me up the road one night. He forced hisself on me. I told him I was a married woman, but he carried on." I couldn't stop now, although I knew I was killing everything between us forever. I should have remembered It's different for men and women.

"I had to get an abortion. I was ill for weeks…" He pushed his chair away from the table and it fell over, causing the waiter to hurry across to us.

"Is there something wrong?" He asked, not daring to come too close to John who had a murderous look about him.

"Get your coat," he ordered me and shoving a handful of money at the waiter, charged out of the restaurant. He was waving down a taxi by the time I caught up with him.

I tried to talk to him all the way home but he wouldn't let me. Just before we reached our close he said, "I'll need to think what to do. I do not want to hear any details. How could you think it was the same as me and that poor German lassie? You're my wife and while I was away there, thinking I might never see you or my weans again, you were getting fucked by a bloody Pole, that probably ran away fae the Germans tae hide here behind the skirts of oor women. And tae have his wean inside ye! I cannae look at you! Don't ever mention it again. I'll tell you when I've decided what to do. I'll sleep on the couch the night."

That was it.

He decided what to do about it a few weeks later. He went back into the army for three years and left me and the weans to start our new life in the Wine Alley without him.

Words can't ever be taken back.

After he went away I felt as if the women in the street were talking about me. They must be thinking I was some woman that couldn't even keep her man, when she did get him back from the war. They never asked, just made sly remarks about him not being able to settle in civvy street and it was a shame he had left me wi' another wean before he left – but that was men, 'man mind thyself' was a true saying, they said, shaking their spiteful heads, but smiling slyly at one another with their eyes.

The weans were great as usual, and most of the time I had plenty of company: Nancy made me laugh, acting like the rich women that came into Olswang and Plottles to buy furs; Vicky was a godsend, helping me make hand-me-downs for the wee ones look not too bad; Conn and Roddy went my messages on a

Saturday (not caring if the other boys thought they were jessies for doing it); Maggie and Billy were out with their pals most of the time. When they were in, she would be lost in a book and he would be drawing – they were no bother. None of my weans were any bother. But I was lonely for somebody my own age to talk to. I began to sit at the close at night with the other women. At first I thought they were going to snub me because I had always kept myself to myself before – John hadn't liked the idea of getting too friendly with them. He was always saying we were a different class and should remember that. But John was in Malaya and I was here in Wine Alley, with no one to talk to, but my weans.

I told them John had been called up again as he was still in the reserves and they seemed to believe me. I didn't care if they did, as long as I was accepted into their coven and allowed to join in the exchange of man-mocking stories; descriptions of horrific 'women's troubles' and the problems of bringing up weans, particularly daughters. They all dreaded their daughters, 'getting in trouble' and drilled it into them not to let boys 'near them' until they were safely married.

Masie Ranachan had given her daughter Sadie an awful slapping one night when her sister Ellen told her that Sadie had been letting a boy 'get a feel' in the back close. The lassie had a bleeding nose and a black eye when she was finished, hitting her, with her auld bachlie shoe she had taken off for the purpose. I felt like greetin' myself as I listened to the poor wee soul' sobs, but the other women egged Maisie on saying that they would do the same if any of their lassies got up to dirty things like that. I didn't know what to think.

I had never even spoken to Nancy and Vicky about things that boys might want to try to do. Nobody had ever told me anything about that kind of thing. I wouldn't know what to say.

My main dread was that somehow they would find out that I had 'got into trouble' and that's why John married me, although he had said it wasn't just that – that he would have married me anyway, though not so soon. He told me years later that his 'real' girlfriend, Mary Stewart, the teacher, was expecting at the same time, but she hadn't told him because she didn't want him to think he was forced to marry her. I never saw her, but I really hated that woman.

The money worries got worse after John went away. His army pay took weeks to come through and I had to get by on the Family Allowance and whatever Nancy and Vicky could give me off their wages.

Mrs Hood, in the next close, talked me into taking a turn in the ménage she ran, and I couldn't pay her. She was such an ugly woman – all treacly brown hair and freckles and teeth that moved when she talked – that I had to force myself to look at her when she came looking for her money. Mind you she brought home-baked cakes for the weans, so I thought she must have some good in her heart: Maybe she would wait a few weeks for the money.

Then there were shoes and clothes for the weans. Vicky and Nancy bought their own stuff, but it meant they had hardly anything left to pay for their keep – but young lasses have to have nice things, so I didn't ask them for much. Conn and Roddy were not hard to please. They had some good shirts and pullovers that Granny Ross had bought them and trousers their dad had bought them before he went away, which just barely covered their ankles. It was Maggie and Billy that were the biggest problem. Maggie was too wee for Nancy and Vicky's cast-offs, although I did manage to turn up some things for her, but Billy refused to go to school in trousers I had altered for him after some rotters laughed at him.

It was John's fault for making them go to that stuck up school. If they had gone to Broomloan Road like the other protestant weans in the street, they wouldn't have looked out of place Everybody wore cast offs there. It wasnae called the 'ragged school' for nothing. Shoes were my biggest worry. Billy could scuff a pair of shoes to death in a week, so I just bought him sandshoes for the dry weather and Mrs Hood gave me a pair of wellies that James had grown out of, for the wet days. He was quite happy with that but he moaned that the teachers were always on at him for not having proper gym shoes and made him take gym in his bare feet. That was another one of the reasons he gave for plunking school – he hated teachers.

*

When John left we'd hardly been speaking – apart from putting on an act for the weans – and he had been edging round me as if he was scared of catching something, but he did warn me not to go near his family. He hated most of them, especially his father Ned and his stepmother Barbara, who never seemed to get out of her bed.

"I don't want you or the weans near them," he said. "They're a bad lot, living like pigs in shit. And don't let them in here either. If they know I'm away they'll try and worm their way in – don't let them."

So I just had to hope he would never find out, when I had to ask Ned for a loan to get shoes for Maggie.

I couldnae ask Granny Ross and hear her saying the same old story about how she had told me John was no good and he would just 'knock weans out of me' and go off and leave me. She ignored the fact that he had left because there was a war on, but he hadn't had that excuse this time and she would be sure to mention that he had added another mouth to feed before he left. She had been scandalised when I fell wi' wee Jay just a month after he came back it was as if there was something disgusting in a man and wife making a wean after they had spent five years away from one another.

Thank god she had never known about the abortion. I would have been more scared of telling her than I had been with John and look how he took it.

*

Wee Maggie was quite taken with her Granda Wales, although I could see she didn't like the way he kept tickling her and sat her on his knee to try on the new shoes. None of my weans have ever liked people touching them. It used to hurt John, the way they cringed away if he tried to give them a cuddle. He said I had made them scared of him, but it wasn't that: I'm not one for cuddling and soppiness – Granny Ross never cuddled me – so they probably got it off me.

It was three weeks before I managed to get the money to pay him back. The army pay came through – with back money – and I bought a big load of messages and treats for everybody, but I put Ned's money aside and went to meet him coming out of work on the Friday night.

I didn't take any of the weans this time. The least they knew the better. They might let slip out to their Daddy some day. I had told Maggie she was to keep the shoes a secret as Daddy didn't like us getting presents from people and she seemed quite happy with that.

The men coming out of the yard were shouting and cheering as I went up to Ned and he pulled me to him in a big hug. I just hoped none of them would ever tell John. He was so well known in Govan and everyone knew Ned was his dad.

"That's the lass," He said, pulling my hand under his arm and squeezing it close to his body. I could smell the dirt off him – not the dirt of work; not oil or sawdust, but body dirt and stale drink and tobacco. I noticed his black nails and thought of John's fussiness about his hands; how it had annoyed him that he never felt clean when he had worked in the gasworks, and with that thought came the realisation of what a terrible thing I was doing in letting his father get a hold over me, I felt sick.

"I'm glad you didnae bring the weans this time," he said. "I can take ye for that wee drink now, eh?"

"I've got to get back," I said, pulling my hand free and taking my purse from my coat pocket. "I just came with your money. John wouldn't like me going into a pub without him."

"Put your purse away lassie," he winked and squeezed me to him. "You don't owe me anything, if I cannae buy a pair of shoes for ma John's wee lass, there's something far wrang. Noo let me show ye off in here." And he swung me through the glass door of The Corner Bar, which was the first stopping off point for most of the shipyard workers on a Friday night – women didn't go in there; not respectable women.

Smoke, oil, wood, metal, bodies and beer made up the mixture of smells that seemed to be tangible in the thick brownish smoke that penetrated my eyes and nose and made the crowd seem to be viewed through opaque glass – the kind you get in lavatory windows. They stood aside to let Ned push me through to a glass-doored cubicle at the far end of the bar – just enough so that I was touched by each and every one of them as I passed – all accidental of course.

There was no one else in the cubicle. It had two dirty tables in front of a bench seat which went into a semi-circle round the partition which separated it from the bar. I felt lost to the world and stupidly wondered if I would ever see my weans again.

"Sit down May ma wee hen; I'll be back in a minute. It's sherry you drink, isn't it?"

He looked, like somebody who had just won the first prize in a raffle, as he winked again and went off to the bar. He was only a few minutes when he came back followed by a man carrying a tray with two drinks on it.

He was like Joe Palooka in the kids comic, or maybe more like Desperate Dan. Everything about him was bulging: his hairy jowls; his chest and above all his enormous tattooed arms, which seemed to be ready to split the shirt sleeves he had rolled up under his oxters. He showed me his brown broken teeth and gave a dirty wink as he put down the drinks on the table – after wiping it with a dirty cloth that had been hanging on his shoulder, being touched by his greasy hair.

"No often we get a decent lassie in here, Ned," he said. "Give us a wave if you want anything else. You'll know be bothered wi' anybody in here." I noticed him looking at my legs and pulled my skirt hem down as far as it would go. He winked again as he went out – this time to Ned.

The sherry was in a 'pony' glass, a much bigger measure than John bought me when we went out. It didn't taste like any sherry I had had before, but it was sweat and pleasant, although it gave me a pain in the back of my neck after it was down and I felt the heat creeping up my body after a couple of mouthfuls.

Ned was sitting too close.

"So our John's left you on your own again," he said shaking his head. "More fool he. I don't know what he's thinking of, leaving a bonnie looking wife like you, to go to the other side of the world. You would think he'd had enough o' the army."

"He had to go," I lied. "He's still a regular soldier. They called him back to his regiment. He'll not be away for too long this time, and I'm not on my own. I've got my weans."

He put his hand on my knee, so softly that I hardly felt it. "Aye but a young, healthy woman needs more than her weans for company," he said and before I could answer: "I'll get us another drink." He stood up and opening the glass door, waved his hand towards the bar. I was sure that the noise in the bar stopped for a minute, as if everyone had drawn a breath at the same time. He sat back down, closer than ever.

"I don't like what you're saying," I choked out. "John wouldn't like what you're saying. My weans were enough for me the last time he was away and I've got one more to look after now. I don't want another drink, here's your money (I threw it on the table) I'm goin' home."

Joe Palooka came in the door just as I stood up to leave.

"Right yar Ned, a wee something for the lassie to eat." He put the tray down, with two drinks and a plate of cream crackers and cheese, making my mouth water; I hadn't tasted crackers and cheese for years.

"Thanks," I tried to smile at him "but you shouldn't have bothered, I'm just going."

"Aw, come on May; don't throw the lad's kindness back in his face," Ned wheedled. "Just this one more drink and I'll walk ye home."

I sat down, making sure that we were not close enough to touch this time and took a gulp of my drink. I felt as if I had been stupid, throwing down the money like that. There was no need for that; He had been kind enough to lend it to me in the first place. I took a crumbly bite of one of the biscuits and knew that I would stay until they were finished – but no more drink, I thought.

He watched me eating, not taking any for himself when I pushed the plate towards him. I wasn't aware of him moving closer or when his arm sneaked across my shoulders. But I felt comfort and warmth seeping into my mind and body and I wanted it to go on.

We had another few drinks, after that. I stopped counting and with each sip I felt less angry and more fond of him. John was always seeing the worst in people; he was just being friendly, trying to be helpful while John was away.

I don't know when his hand had crept under my skirt. I was lying back on the bench, laughing at something he said – he was very very witty – when I felt him trying to loosen my suspenders. The horrible thing was that I was enjoying him touching me. I wanted to lie back there and let him do what he liked. I wanted to forget that anyone could walk in on us or look over the partition. I wanted to forget about John and the weans. I wanted to be stroked and petted like a cat on heat.

It was his smell as he moved closer (in for the kill, I thought) that woke me up. This time I didn't hesitate, I ran out of that pub like a dose of salts, trying not to hear the laughing and crude comments.

He didn't follow me. If he had he would never have caught up. I didn't stop running until I got back to number sixteen. I was glad the weans were all in bed, when I looked at my scarlet face in the mirror. I looked like one of these drunk women you see on street corners, asking men to buy them more drinks, for God knows what in return.

For weeks after that night, I jumped every time the door went and always made sure I answered it myself, in case some of the weans would open it and let their Granda Wales in.

Apart from the fear, my worst feeling was shame at what I had nearly done. The thought tormented me night and day, that the touch of a man's hand (even my repulsive father-in-law's) could make me want to act like a tart. I wanted John back; he should never have left me again. The weans were not enough for me. I had always thought that nice women shouldn't need all that sex business, the way men did, but, to my shame, I realised that I did.

Apart from dreading every knock on the door, I felt that nothing was going right since John left. Vicky had taken up wi' that catholic fella from next door. It made me sick to see them together – her always turned out perfectly, even though she hadn't a lot of fancy clothes, and him, looking like a dirty tinker in his wellington boots with his trousers tucked into them, and a polo necked jumper, even when they were going out to the pictures – but she was determined, and I couldn't stop her.

I could stop her becoming catholic though. That's one thing I could never thole and I knew her daddy would feel the same.

When she said she was going to marry him and she had written to John to tell him, I just laughed at her. I knew what he would say: He didn't exactly say 'no' but he told her to wait until he came home and then he would give her a 'big white wedding'. At first, when she told me his answer, I was raging. Then, when I had time to think, I knew what he was up to – there were no flies on John Wallace – I just smiled to myself. He was sure she would come her senses and see Big Terry for what he was, if she had to wait two years, until he came home.

When I saw what she was hiding in her room, I knew his plan was not working!

Our Maggie was standing there with these papish baubles round her neck and her wee pal was holding the fancy prayer book, with a picture of that catholic whore on it, when I went into the room to see what they were up to, I drew my hand across Maggie's jaw and told the two of them to get outside. I put the filth in the pocket of my overall.

My face felt as if it was on fire for the rest of the day, waiting for Vicky to come home and explain what was going on – I knew fine well.

That night, after she had run out crying and the rest of the weans had gone to bed, there was still a wee bright green flame, shooting out occasionally from the dying fire, as if it was defying me and every so often a bead would shoot onto the hearth as if it had been fired from a pea-shooter.

Well, I had shown her there would be no papish rubbish in my house. The prayer book and the rosary had made a good blaze and I hoped it had burned home the message that she could stop taking instruction to become a catholic, if she wanted to be a part of this family. What would John say, or do, if he came back to find his daughter was a catholic? What would Granny Ross think? I had done the right thing. She wouldn't try anything like that again and maybe it would put him off marrying her altogether, for his family would not want him to marry a protestant.

*

John wrote more to the weans than he did me. He sent the younger ones photos of the wonderful sights he was seeing in Singapore and India and Nancy and Vicky silk suits and the boy's hand-painted ties. He sent me presents too, but he never mentioned anything important between us in his letters. Maybe he had decided to forget what I had told him about the Pole and everything would be all right when he came home.

He had been away just two years when I decided to pour my heart out to him, I wrote:

Dear John,

The weans and I are all doing fine. Vicky, Nancy and Conn are all working hard at their jobs. Vicky's still seeing that big clown next door, but I think she might be going off him. Roddy's doing well at school. His teacher wrote me a letter saying he is University material. Maggie's at the big school – in the top class, and Billy is more settled now. Wee John is running around and into everything. They will all be writing to you to thank you for the presents, but it's not them I really want to talk about in this letter John. It's us – as man and wife. I know you said you never wanted to talk about what I told you about what happened to me while you were away, but I'm begging you to let me explain, so that we can put this behind us. I love you as much as I did when you first asked me out. You're the only boyfriend I ever had John. You know that. Don't let one stupid mistake, and it was a mistake, spoil our whole lives. I was lonely when you were away and then I got that telegram saying you were missing – presumed dead. John for six months I didn't know if I was a widow or not, whether I would ever see you again. I didn't know if the weans still had a daddy.

It was on the day that I heard that you were alive – in a prisoner of war camp, but alive – that the terrible thing happened.

I took Nancy and Vicky, in turns to the pictures on a Friday night. That night it was Nancy's turn. It was a musical and we were singing all the songs as we walked up through the blackout. Nothing could have spoiled the way I felt that night. You were alive. You would be coming back to us. We were just cutting through the farm, past the barn when one of the Polish prisoners started to walk along side with us. I had worked beside him when we were all helping to bring in the hay and he seemed a really nice bloke – quite old for a soldier, and he told me about his wife and family back home and how he was scared he would never see them again. I was quite pleased to see him because it was dark and Nancy was scared. He gave her a pick-a-back the rest of the way to our door and I sent her in to put the kettle on for our supper and stood talking to him outside. There was a wee outhouse kind of place just outside the door, where Menzies, the farmer, kept some bales of dry hay for the cattle.

We were leaning against the door. I was telling him my good news about you. I don't know yet how it happened, but suddenly we were inside with the door shut. It was pitch black, but I could hear him, kind of sobbing and he was holding me so tight I couldn't get away. I nearly shouted for the boys but I didn't want them to see me in there with a strange man. He did it to me John and just walked away and left me there. I gave in. He was too strong for me. I was too tired to fight. I never told anybody about it until that night I told you – apart from the woman who helped me to get the baby done away with. I thought you would understand what it was like when you told me about the German girl. A lot of women had weans to other men while their men were away and they're bringing them up as their own. I'm not saying that's right John, but everything was different then. People did things they would never do at another time, I wouldn't even recognise that Pole if he turned up on the doorstep tomorrow, John. He meant nothing to me, but I would like to think that his wife would understand why he did such a thing – if she was still alive when he got home.

I don't know what else I can tell you John to make you understand and forgive me. I want us to go back to the way we were before I told you. Please say we will.

Your loving wife May xxxxxx

It was a month before a letter came from him for me. There were letters in between addressed to Vicky and Nancy (she had written to tell him she was joining the WRAAF) but nothing for me. When it did come, I waited until they were all in bed at night, before I took it out of my apron pocket and read it. It was the worst letter I ever read in my life.

Dear May,

I'm writing to tell you for the last time that I don't want to get any more letters like the last one you sent. I don't want to hear the filthy details about how you got another man's wean inside you. It doesn't make any difference. You keep saying it was just the same with me and the German lass, well it was entirely different. You're my wife and I should have been able to trust you. The German lass was different, she had no weans and her man hadn't been heard of for years. You had a family to look after and you knew I would be coming back to you, it's no use, I've tried and tried to accept what you did, but I can't get you with that Pole out of my head. He was the enemy and you let him inside you to plant a wee bastard in the same place I had been in; the same place my weans come from. I'll never be able to forget that. I'll not desert you and the weans. When I come back from here it'll be for good, well until they're all grown up. I'm their daddy and I'll stay with you and them. If I left, what would you tell them? I hope they will never know the terrible thing you did. I always want them to look up to you and respect you as their mother. How could they if they knew what you had done. We'll go on living together May but never again as man and wife. Don't mention this in your letters again; I'll stop writing if you do.

John.

I drew my chair closer to the fire, knowing I would get 'corn beef legs'. "The sign of a lazy woman," John used to say, but what did it matter now. He couldn't think any worse of me than he did. My legs and hands were burning as I crouched over the fire like a witch over her cauldron, but inside I was frozen to the bone and aching from the effort to make myself small enough to hide from my own hatred and disgust. I saw now that he was right. What I had done had been a terrible thing and I couldn't blame anyone but myself.

The soldier hadn't raped me. He'd been a wee bit rough but I had wanted him to do it as much as he wanted to do it. We had just been two animals, doing what nature makes animals do. I couldn't blame the war or the loneliness (I had the weans) and millions of other women had not cheated on their men when they were away – it was only the sluts, like me, that had done that.

*

At least he was coming home and nobody would ever know what I had done to him. I crumpled the letter up and threw it on the fire and as it flared up I let a wee flame of hope light in my heart – maybe John would be able to forgive me in time.

*

Maggie's Memory

They were glad in a way he had left, although none of them said so. They breathed easier somehow. May was a bit sad and snappy for a few days, and kept her curlers in, just covering her head with a headscarf when she went to the shops or took wee Jay for his walk. It didn't last.

She just shrugged herself back to life and carried on as she had done before he came home, but now she had a new baby and a new house to keep her busy, along with the six other weans he had left her with, now growing up too fast for her liking. The summer nights were coming in, when the women would be sitting at the close mouth or leaning on their window sills, gossiping and laughing; the younger, more daring ones sometimes taking part in the street games. May had never joined in before.

"A bunch o' lazy women, sitting slandering their neighbours," Johnnie had said. "It would fit them better to attend to their houses and weans. I wouldnae like to see any wife o' mine sitting around a close – like bloody witches around a cauldron."

The house was empty most nights, apart from her and wee Jay, until bedtime: Vicky and Nancy were out with pals or boyfriends; Conn and Roddy were involved in whatever game was going on in the street and Maggie and Billy were sitting on the civer, spectating and hoping she would forget to call them in for their bed.

She felt her face burn as she got a plaid from the bedroom and wrapped the baby in it. The women looked at her as she emerged from the close mouth and she felt like turning and going back up the stairs, until a voice said from somewhere on the right of the group, " Move up and let the lassie in, you lot, there's plenty o' room." The words were spoken by Maisie Ranachan, of all people. Her bedroom window was just next to the close and she was sitting there, like a Buddha in the mouth of a cave, leaning on three layers for comfort – a pillow from her bed, her white dimpled arms and the over-flowing clootie dumplings of her breasts. She sat there nearly every night, from about eight o'clock until well after dark, overseeing the rituals of the close. The other women listened when she spoke, asked her advice and treated her with a kind of awed respect, tingled with fear.

She had a rival for supremacy, who was equally respected, but more feared, Mamie Watson – she of the hairy face, also did sentry duty at her window, on the first floor, so that they were sort of diagonally opposed to one another. Her pronouncements had the advantage of coming from above, also she could see more of what was going on than Maisie and sometimes yelled at some young couple having a fumble in the darkness of one of the closes opposite, to, "Get out o' that, you filthy slut!". It was never the boy or the man who was verbally abused, always the female. In her philosophy it was the male right, "To get their candy where they could."

May did not stay long that first night. She didn't want the wean out too long in the night air, but she was closely questioned while she was there and answered every question openly and naively. Her answers provided fodder for sympathetic noises from the other women until it was time to go in and for mouth-watering conversations after she was gone.

It became routine. She said it helped to get wee Jay off to sleep. She would sit there until nine o'clock – laughing, red-faced at the crude jokes and exposing all her money worries and private things to the nest of women, waiting open-mouthed to guzzle more of her secrets and regurgitate them later – and then call Maggie and Billy for bed, and go upstairs, taking up her post at the window, once they were in bed. She felt daring, elated and guilty at her involvement with the 'close women' as she thought of them. She never spoke from the window, feeling it was not her place to do so, just watched and listened, until it was time for Conn and Roddy to come in, usually after dark.

*

The differences between May and the other women at the close were not just due to her age, although she was several years younger, it was her looks, her man being away and her shyness and naiveté. She knew very little about them, they knew almost everything about her. She was like a little girl mixing with grown up women.

*

Billy and I used to sneak up in the semi-darkness and watch and listen. It seemed to us that the women sometimes made a fool of her, and she didn't know it. She just laughed along with them when they sniggered at some foolishness of hers, she told them about. Like arriving home without the pram, (with wee Jay in it) having left it outside the shops and having to run back in a panic; or putting coloureds in her wash, so that everything came out pink: "Even John's best shirt!" she told them.

We felt that they were jealous of her because they were all so ugly. They wore hairnets, or curlers, or both. While her black hair was loose and straight apart from curling up at the ends, on her cheeks, (the result of only two curlers, she put in before going to bed at night). She sometimes looked about twelve, with her grey eyes sparkling and her cheeks flushed, as she listened to the telling of some bedtime experience of one of her new friends. Few of them there weighed less than three times her weight and wrapped in the tartan plaid, with her baby in her arms, she looked like an illustration for a Burns poem. She was the glamour and romance in the close. She even wore powder and lipstick when she took Billy and me to the pictures some Friday nights.

*

The other women despised her; were fascinated by her and missed her if she did not turn up at the close mouth coven. She was lonely at times. She felt that she lacked the status of a married woman. The biggest part of her days was spent with the baby, the rest of the family being at school or work. In the evenings they only stopped in long enough to be fed and were off again into their own lives, independent of her, but the loneliness was not the worst thing – that was the lack of money.

Having an Army pay book gave her an importance in the eyes of the other women. They saw it as having her man's unopened pay packet every week – something they had never experienced – but it did not stretch any further than their money and as the months went by and she got involved in, *'Provi Cheques', 'Ménages'* and other forms of 'tick'. She found that she had to pay most of it out as soon as she lifted it from the Post Office. The same was true of her Family Allowance. It all went on food, there was nothing left for emergencies and sometimes – worst humiliation' she had to borrow coins for the gas meter, until pay day.

*

Billy and I had been playing at jumping over puddles, on the way home from school, which became pushing one another into the slimy backcourt water, until our legs, socks and shoes all had the same soggy, black appearance. It was a great game and culminated, hysterically in squelching like the 'Monster from the Black lagoon', all the way through the close and up the stairs, making us laugh until pee trickled down my legs to mingle with the black slime. One of my shoes had become like an open mouth, with mud-coloured toes sticking out, like some obscene tongue. Every time I flapped the jaws up and down, Billy held his stomach with laughter pains. Our childish minds thought that Mammy would enjoy the joke when we walked into the kitchen.

She didn't!

She was angry enough about the mess, swinging at the two of us with the dish towel she was holding, but it was the sight of my shoe, gaping and waggling at her that made her fly at me and, holding me with one hand, slap me first on one cheek and then the other, until I really did hear ringing in my ears.

"What are ye goin' to wear on ye feet now? You stupid wee bitch!" she yelled at me as I backed away from her into the lobby – tears and snotters tripping me, wee Jay began to scream; I wailed and Billy grinned, as he always did when he was scared, sorry or embarrassed. I don't know what would have happened next – child murder maybe – if suddenly a loud angry knocking had not started on the floor beneath our feet.

Maisie Ranachan had saved my life. This was how she told us we were making too much noise for her liking. I'm sure her ceiling must have been covered in dents, because she chapped up to us several times most days.

Mammy tried to fix the shoe. She cleaned it up and squeezed some rubber solution the boys had for mending footballs, and left it all night under the weight of the flat iron, only to see it opening its 'mouth' in a yawn when she removed the weight in the morning. She laughed and we all joined in, relieved that her anger had passed. "I'll have to keep you off school till I get you a pair of shoes," she sighed.

"Can I stay off too?" Billy was quick to spot the opportunity for a holiday, but she had had letters from the school about his 'absences' and did not want any more.

"You can wear the sandshoes, until I get you a pair of boots," she said.

The sandshoes were a pair of black gym shoes which Billy and I shared for the PT periods at school. Luckily we never got the subject at the same time. It was decided that Billy would take a note on gym days to say that his sandshoes were too small and he would have a new pair soon, in the meantime: 'I'll be obliged if he can be excused gym', Mammy said in the note.

That note gave Miss Dorian a lot of pleasure. "You can stay in class and practice your arithmetic master Wallace," she sneered, "Until your mother can afford to equip you properly for school." Billy tossed his head and whinnied like a horse when he demonstrated to me how she had said this. He was not scared of her anymore, since the end of the 'ruler torture'.

*

May decided to go and see Granda Wallace.

Johnnie had never made him welcome in their home, since the early days of their marriage, when they had lived in one room in his Uncle John's house and he had warned her not to have anything to do with his family, but: "He was always fond o' the weans," she told herself. Whenever she had run into him, he had always made a fuss of them, giving them the loose change from his pockets, or buying them ice cream. He had never visited them since Johnnie came home. She knew there was something unforgiven between them. She guessed it was something to do with the death of Johnnie's mother and his re-marriage to a

Catholic woman. 'nothing better than a tink'. She just knew that he despised his father and hated his stepmother. She knew also that he would not forgive her going to them for help, but he did not need to know. That was what she thought, as she got herself and wee Jay ready to go and meet her father-in-law, when he came out of work in the yards.

When the hooter sounded and the huge metal gates opened, the men rushed out of the shipyards, like smoke spewing from a chimney, their faces and clothes all the same, oily grey colour, topped with bonnets that seemed welded to their heads. She hoped none of them recognised her as Johnnie Wallace's wife, as she stood there, gripping onto the handle of the go-chair – bought with the last Provi cheque and still to be paid for.

Some of the men nudged each other and winked and laughed at her, one even shouting: "Yer too early for pay night, hen. Come on, a'll buy ye a drink!"

She wanted to shout back some smart answer, but instead she busied herself fixing the baby's cover, feeling her face burning, praying again that nobody would recognise her. She was about to turn and run off, when one of the grey figures grabbed her arm: "May, what are you doing here? Has something happened to Johnnie?" Ned held onto her, peering into her face, ignoring the cheers of his workmates and their remarks:

"Hi, auld yin. She a wee bit young fer ye."

"Have you been keepin' secrets from your mates?"

"Ye sly auld bastard!".

He held up his free hand to them and they were quiet, going on their way laughing and shaking their heads in admiration that an old man like Ned would be met by a young 'bit o' stuff' and a wean as well.

"I just brought wee Jay to see his Granda," she told him as they walked away from the gates. "You've never seen him since he was born."

"A didnae think a wid be welcome. You know what Johnnie's like." He took the handle of the pram from her. "Come on, we'll go for a cuppa tea. A cannae take ye fer a drink wi' the wean. We'll go in tae the Grand Cafe. Ye should have come to the hoose. It's embarrassing for a man – a woman meeting him fae his work."

"I never thought," she answered. "The truth is Ned. I need tae ask you for help and I don't want anybody else tae know about it. Johnnie would kill me if he knew." They didn't speak again until they were seated in a booth in the cafe, with cups of tea and a plate of chocolate biscuits in front of them – and a 'pokey hat' for wee Jay.

"Right lass," he said, patting her knee under the table. "What's the matter?" She moved further back on the bench, her cheeks flushing up. She had forgotten what he was like for touching. Now she remembered Johnnie telling him to 'Keep his hands to hisself', when he had visited them in the rented rooms they stayed in before the war. But Johnnie had always been so touchy about things like that, that she felt a bit sorry for his father, who had only given her waist a friendly squeeze. She hadn't seen any harm in it. "Take it from me," Johnnie had said. "He's a dirty auld bugger – always pawin' about women. He's lucky I don't banjo him. Don't you ever let him in here when I'm no' in. Mind!"

She screwed the memory into a ball and threw it away. Best not to think about it.

"I need a loan of some money, just a couple o' pound," she said, taking a gulp of the hot tea and feeling her tongue burn.

"Loan!" he laughed. "Loan, from your wean's Granda? You'll be getting no loan fae me! Anything you need, ye'll get an' It'll be givin' gladly." He had moved forwards so that their knees were touching beneath the table and she couldn't move any further back in the bench.

"It's our Maggie," she explained. "She needs shoes. Her shoes are done, I'll pay ye back when Johnnie's money comes through."

He shook his head. "Ye'll do no such thing." He took a huge dirty hanky from his pocket – she could sell the stale tobacco from it – and wiped the ice cream dribbles from wee Jay's chin. May knew she had made a mistake in coming to him for help. He was everything Johnnie hated. God help her if he ever found out that she had asked for help from this man – Granda or not!

"The morra night is pay night," he was saying, holding out a black finger for the baby to grasp. "You bring wee Maggie to meet me here an' I'll take ye tae buy her a pair of shoes. Eh? How's that? It'll be a secret between the two o' us, an' It'll gie me a chance tae meet anither wan o' ma grand-weans. What age is she now?"

"She's nearly ten," she answered, and then (hoping it would never happen) "What time will I meet you?"

"The same time as the night," he answered. "A go for a pint after work, so naebody will be any the wiser, if I'm late hame.

It was arranged. She couldn't get out of it, she told herself, but this would be the last. She would pay him back out of next week's pay and she wouldn't need to see him again.

They went in different directions when they left the cafe and she began to feel quite happy as she wheeled the pram home. She had been like a stupid wee lassie to imagine he was deliberately touching her and the hanky was probably just discoloured from being in his pocket. A wee bit dirt didnae do weans any harm, they said.

At least Maggie would get her shoes.

*

After she had a night to think about it – facing Johnnie's wrath in her dreams – she dreaded meeting Ned the next day and Maggie didn't help by talking non-stop about the kind of shoe she would like.

"There'll be no fancy straps or buckles," she snapped. "You'll take what you get; something plain and heard wearing for school. And get that hair out of your eyes, before we go anywhere. You look like a tinker wean."

Maggie was not listening. She was picturing herself in a pair of red leather shoes, with an ankle strap, or maybe black patent, with a side-buckle fastening. One of the toffs in her class had a pair like that and she could picture the looks, if she turned up with a pair the same.

*

Maggie's Memory

It was the first time I had met Granda Wallace – or the first I remembered anyway – and he didn't live up to my expectations: I had imagined a tall, handsome man; an older version of Daddy, but with dark hair, instead of auburn. He did have a handsome face, with very fine features and light blue eyes, which had a fly look about them, but he was not that much taller than Conn, and looked as if needed a shave. His trousers were baggy and shiny, and his shirt collar thick with black grease, which seemed to have spilled over from his neck. His pockets were crammed full of sweeties, when he met us outside the shoe shop and he kept offering me my pick from a paper poke, while the shoe-buying was going on. They had a strong tobacco flavour – whether they were peardrops (my favourite) or black striped balls, which I did not like at first, but grew accustomed to.

He seemed to know the woman who served us in the shop really well as he patted her bottom every time she was close enough and she went red and giggled, saying, "You're an awful man, Ned Wallace, behave yourself."

Mammy told her to bring, 'sensible shoes, in black, size two' and he laughed and said to me, "What kind of shoes dae ye want, wee hen Its you that's got to wear them, no yer Mammy."

"I would like a strap, Granda," I said, ignoring Mammy's glare. "That's what all the other lassies at my school are wearing, so it is."

"Bring every shoe in the shop, in my granddaughters size, wi' a strap, ye wee smasher," he instructed the girl, giving her waist a squeeze that made her go as scarlet and ready to burst as an over-ripe tomato.

Eventually Mammy gave in and allowed me to have a pair of brown shoes with a strap across the instep and a button fastening at the side. She dug her heels in about the colour – I had wanted red or blue. I could see she was getting annoyed at the way Granda had let me choose my own shoes, insisting on trying them on me, lifting my leg and foot up, sometimes resting it on the top of his leg as he pushed the shoe on, twisting my wee skinny leg this way and that as he admired the fit or the colour. I was dying with embarrassment as I was sure everyone in the shop could see my knickers as he did this. But I would have put up with anything to get those shoes.

"Right, that's it," she said, standing up and angrily shaking the go-chair, in which wee Jay was beginning to whinge and looking as if she was itching to slap someone – probably me. "We'll have the brown pair. This wean needs changing and the rest of them will be waiting for their tea." To the girl: "She'll wear them – ye dinna need a box."

Ned insisted on buttoning my feet into the new shoes, resting them between his legs as he did so. I suddenly felt sick and ashamed – not knowing why.. I understood when I looked back on the experience as a grown-up, and realising that even Grandas have bad things inside, that sometimes get the better of them.

*

At least Maggie had a decent pair of shoes to wear to school. May shrugged her distaste of Ned's behaviour from her mind. She'd probably been seeing too much into it. It was just his fun.

When the next week came, she could not pay the shoe money back as she'd promised herself she would. By the time she had paid the rent, bought Billy a second hand jacket for school and paid her ménage to Mrs Hood up the next close, she had hardly anything left of her Army pay and the Family Allowance was needed for food and money for the gas meter. She never seemed to have enough money left over to pay the debt and dreaded running into Ned, or him coming to the house. Every time she looked at Maggie's shoes, which were scuffed and broken within a month, she promised herself they would be paid off from the next pay. She thought about missing paying Mrs Hood, but she was more scared of her than of Ned. Once before she had missed a payment and had had a visit from her.

*

Maggie's Memory

I remember it was me who had opened the door to her. The first thing I noticed was that she was carrying a cloth-covered plate, which smelt of those wee home bakeries you used to see down the back streets of most Scottish towns – a mixture of hot butter, sugar and ripe apples that made you sniff the air like a Bisto kid. I had to slurp quickly to stop the slavers running down my chin. Already we had heard that Mrs Hood was a great baker, I thought this must be a kind of 'good neighbour' – bringing us a sample – apple tart or wee soft, fat scones, with juicy raisins snuggling in them, that silently squeaked when you bit into them.

The second thing I noticed was her freckles. In most freckly people, the freckles stand out like spots shaken from a paintbrush, against the white skin, but with her, it was the white skin that stood out – there was so little of it among the freckles.

"She's just one big freckle," Billy said to me as we stood in the kitchenette, staring at the covered plate. She was in the living room talking to Mammy. It was mainly her voice we heard, menacing sounds without words, then with sudden friendly clarity as Mammy walked her to the door. "A'm sure ye man widnae be pleased to hear from me," she said, as the door shut. "Enjoy the cakes."

Mammy's face was pure white when she came into the kitchen. "Auld two-faced bitch," she said. "Comin' here wi' her cakes. I've a good mind tae throw them in the fire." Billy and I grabbed them at the same time, knocking the cloth off to reveal – butterfly-cakes! They were not going into the fire. The slavers in our mouths were sure about that.

"Oh, OK." The colour had come back into her cheeks. "We'll have one each w' a wee fly cuppa tea." She laughed like a wee girl enjoying doing something, she knew she shouldn't do. "No use wasting good cakes. Put the kettle on Maggie."

At times like that I loved her so much, it made me feel like crying. When we were sitting at the living room fire, with our tea and cakes, she explained to us what it was all about. We were only nine and ten years old, but she told us things that most people would only tell an adult: It turned out that she had missed her ménage payments two weeks in a row and Mrs Hood, who ran it, had said she would get in touch with Daddy's regiment if she did not pay the arrears and promise not to miss paying again. May pictured her man being called out of the ranks and told in front of everyone that his wife was in debt. All that worried her was how angry he would be and how stupid he would think her. Mrs Hood had to be paid.

"If we have to live on bread and marge for a week," she told us as we licked the butter cream off Mrs Freckle's cake.

"What is a ménage anyway?" Conn asked, when the story was repeated to him and Roddy, when they came in.

"It's like…" her face flushed and she wiped wee Jay's face vigorously as if she was polishing the brasses, "It's a group of people, all putting in so much money a week, and getting their turn of getting stuff out of the warehouse – like sheets and towels and things. Mine is the last turn, so I haven't got anything yet, but if one person misses paying, the person that's running it, that's Mrs Hood, has to make up the money." She was as confused as us, but all the other women at the close were 'taking a turn', so she had joined to save face. Poverty had to be kept as secret as possible.

"Why do they call it a ménage?" Roddy asked. "It sounds like a kind of zoo – a menagerie." This made us all laugh in admiration of his cleverness and we forgot all about the prospect of bread and marge for a week, as we relished the rest of 'Mrs Freckle's' cakes. Billy had given Mrs Hood a new name.

*

It was not only the overpopulation of her skin by freckles, that was strange about Mrs Hood/Freckle's: Her marriage also had something off about it. Her man was known as 'Jackie Easton' – not Hood and seemed to live with her and their big family on an irregular basis. All of the family were redheads, suffering the freckle affliction to various degrees, from speckled bird's egg through oatmeal, to the invasion of the freckle hordes on their mother's skin, yet Jackie was a ruddy complexioned redhead, without a little brown spot in sight.

He was another one of the mysteries that we were discovering all the time in the Wine Alley and Billy and I had him down as 'a man on the run from the police' who only dared to come home now and again when the 'coast was clear'.

*

Every day of the week, after that first visit, Mrs Freckle arrived at the door, always with a covered plate exuding a tormenting smell – sometimes it was pancakes, others her famous jam buns: always it was just before tea, when we were starving.

I had this fantasy about her being like the witch in Hansel and Gretel, tempting us to eat her baking, so that she could capture us and keep us in a cage, to be fattened up for 'the kill'. But nothing could have stopped me from eating them. We looked forward to her visits, shutting our ears to her hints to Mammy about 'paying your dues'. The day before the army pay was due she was particularly generous with her cakes – butterflies again – which flew off the plate and into our mouths in seconds, the icing sugar which coated them, spurting out in a sweet haze on our breath. She stayed longer that day as well, saying to Mammy, "Could ye send the weans out tae play. A want tae tell ye somethin'." I dawdled, tying my shoelaces, hoping they wouldn't notice me and I would hear what she had to say, but Mammy shooed me off and shut the living room door. Her face was whiter than the icing on the cakes.

*

She poked her head out the door, to make sure the weans had really gone out – that wee Maggie was a nosey wee bitch, too auld for her age, and what she had to say was not for spreading around the street.

"Ye don't need tae have 'this worry every week ye know'," she began, showing off her white teeth in a friendly smile, and shaking her head so that a greasy strand of her treacle-toffee coloured hair coiled itself out of her hairnet of the same colour. May foutered with the ties on her apron. She felt that something awful was about to be said and realised how scared she was of this woman.

"There's ways of getting money tae tide you over. A've helped ither people."

"What do you mean?" May asked, wishing she would just go away.

"There's such a thing as a loan – jist tae clear yer feet and gie ye a fresh start," she said – smiling horribly again.

"I couldn't pay back a loan." May got up and started clearing the table. She didn't know why she felt so scared. "I'm sorry I ever took the ménage. I just thought it would be a good way of getting new sheets and things. We've been using the ones I've had since we were married." She felt ashamed. "But John would go mad if he knew I was in debt. He would never let me get a loan of money, anyway, surely you need security – do you not? No I've given you your ménage money and I'll go on paying it every week, even if the weans have to do without. I'll maybe try to get somebody to take over my turn, eh?"

"Ye could pay the whole thing if ye goat a loan and huv plenty left for ither things yer weans need," Mrs Hood tempted.

A picture came into her mind of new clothes for all the family; doing up the living room and maybe even getting a new coat for herself. She felt as if she had the money in her purse already and wished the woman would hurry up and go before she couldn't stop herself giving in. John would never forgive her if she did. Yet, in her mind she was making a list, as if she already had the money.

"You're man dismal need tae know and you've goat the Family Allowance book – huv ye no?"

"What's that got to do with it?" Suddenly May felt her purse emptying again.

"That's yer security. That's how ither women get loans. The lender keeps ye book an' gies ye it back when the loan's paid. It's simple. Nae forms tae sign or anything – just the counterfoil in yer book every week. The mair Family Allowance you get the mair money you can borrow."

*

Maggie

"It sounds so easy." She said to us later, "I told her I would think about it. What dae you think, Vicky?" (Vicky was the clever one of the family).

"I think there must be a catch. I don't like that woman, she looks like a really fly person to me."

"What's in it for her?" Conn put in.

"Maybe she just wants to help," Mammy answered. We were not saying what she wanted to hear. "She's been good to us – bringing us home baking and waiting for her ménage money, even though it put her out of pocket. It would be nice to be able to buy a lot of new things. Look at the holes in our Billy's jersey. There's hardly a bit left to sew!"

"Well I just don't think you should get in tow with anybody in this street. They're scruffs! What about the woman's man? He's got a different name from her and the family is ignorant. They shout and whistle every time I pass them." Vick gave her final verdict, which was based strictly on selfish reasons. Why should she care if her wee brother looked like a rag bag – as long as none of her friends at work ever saw him.

"And they're pot ugly!" Billy and I said together.

"You don't think her cakes are ugly though," Mammy was getting angry with us.

She wanted the things that that money would buy for us and see them disappearing in our refusal to see the loan as a good thing.

"Anyway," she poked madly at the fire. "She asked us could all down for our tea tomorrow night. A don't suppose any o' you will want tae go, if she's such a fly horrible person."

"I didnae say she was fly," Billy said. "A want to go, a like Robert Hood – he's mad."

"A'm goin' as well," I said. "A play wi' Flora. She's got quite nice hair." A lie, it looked like rusty straw.

Nothing would persuade the four oldest of us to go; Vicky for snobbish reasons; Nancy because she didn't miss the dancing for anything and Conn and Roddy because they thought going to somebody's house for your tea was 'sissy' and 'sissy' was the worst thing anyone could be.

We were to be there for six o'clock, so I started getting ready around three. I got Nancy to put curlers in my hair. She wasn't too keen because Billy and I had a letter from the school nurse a few weeks before, warning that we had 'a few nits'; "Which must be eradicated immediately, for the sake of the other children as well as themselves." And mammy had been washing our hair every night in something called 'Derback soap' which was black and smelt like public lavatories. Anyway the metal curlers went in, pulling my scalp so tight in places, that I had slanty eyes for a while. The next thing was my shoes. I polished them until the uppers looked like new – the heels were already wedge shaped with wear, but Mammy had bought me a pair of white socks, so I thought the worn out heels would not be noticed in the overall dazzling effect. Then I sneaked in and borrowed a pair of white knickers from Vicky's drawer and a fluffy jumper from Nancy's – My school skirt would have to do; it was the only one I had – oh, and a chiffon scarf that I had seen Vicky tie in a bow at the side of her neck. I practiced tying it for ages, but one of the ends persisted in sticking up, when it should lie down. I stuck a couple of hankies inside my vest, to give me a bust and prayed they wouldn't move. I smirked and preened in front of the wardrobe mirror in the 'big' room for at least half-and-hour after Nancy had frizzed out my hair. Some of it hadn't turned out right, so I had straight lanky stands among the curls, which Nancy skewered to my head with Kirby grips, to hide them under the frizz.

I was pleased with the effect, and couldn't take my eyes off my blonde-haired legs above the white socks and shiny shoes, apart from when I sneaked into the room to have another smirk and preen at my reflection. I was practicing a new smile, copied from a picture in 'Red Star Weekly' and didn't want to use it in public, until it was ready.

By five o'clock, I was ready and given the job of amusing wee Jay, while Mammy got herself ready and 'scraped some o' the tottlies' out of Billy's ears. This was her way of saying that there was so much dirt in them that potatoes might grow there. I enjoyed the picture that came into my mind of Billy with bushy green potato plants coming out of his ears, but my enjoyment did not last long. Wee Jay wanted that scarf off my neck and began to scream with insane delight as he scrabbled his little fingers at it, until I was nearly strangled. There was only one thing to do – I waited until no one was looking and gave his soft, milky-looking arm a good pinch. He let go the scarf and looked from me to the arm, with a sort of 'what did you do that for?' look, and then pushed out his 'petted-lip' and looked desperately around for his mother, who was busy 'tatty-howking'. Before he could go on to the next part of his baby repertoire – sobbing broken heartedly – I lifted him up and shoogled and tickled him until he laughed shamelessly, the scarf and pinch forgotten.

The Hoods were already sitting at a long table in the living room when we arrived, apart from Mrs Freckle herself, and – disappointingly for Billy and I, no Jackie Easton. The smell of baking nearly made me faint. I had never seen such a food-laden table. At that moment I loved Mrs Freckle and wished I was a

Hood. I looked at Billy. He had a totally mad grin on his face and I noticed his teeth were watering. For once in his life he forgot to be shy.

"Right, you two, sit in there between oor Flora and Robert," Mrs Freckle told us and we bumped into each other in our keenness to obey. She laughed. "Don't worry, there's plenty for everybody. You sit here beside me May and ye can put the wee yin in this high chair – mine are a' too auld fer it now."

That meal was not only the most delicious I ever ate, it was the strangest. The behaviour of the Hood family would have been enough to put anybody off, but not us, we were too hungry/greedy? Every time we helped ourselves from the plates of sausage rolls, sandwiches, cakes etc, they nudged each other, exchanging winks and nods of the head, even laughing outright when their mother asked: "Well, are you enjoying your tea?" They ate as much as us but their attention was on us, rather than the food. It could have been off-putting, but not to us

Ellen, the second eldest daughter – a scrawny lassie, who looked as if somebody had started out to make Rita Hayworth, but got all the features in the wrong size and place, had just been sent to get more food from the kitchen, but she came back empty handed, with her freckles standing out like bristles on her white cheeks.

"It's m' da!" she cried, looking at her mother in terror.

"Quick intae the room!" I could see Mrs Freckle's hands shaking as she began to gather up plates and cups, carelessly squashing the unfinished food, mixing apple tarts, with sausage rolls and sandwiches with butterfly cakes.

I felt like snatching them from her but Flora had hold of my arm and was dragging me towards the door, saying, "Into the room, quick!"

We were pushed and pulled through the bedroom door which, the same as in our house, was next to the outside door. I looked at Billy, just before the door opened and he was grinning manically. A sound between a giggle and a rift spurted from me. I didn't know which to fear more – going into the room, or being caught by the sinister Jack Easton – who had become like 'Blind Pugh' in my imagination.

"Ah cannae see," it was Billy's voice.

"Sssssssshh!" There seemed to be about a hundred voices making the air wet with their instructions to keep quiet.

"Put the light on," I pleaded.

"There's no bulb." I think it was Robert Hood who answered, but I was too taken up with pain to care. I had just stubbed my toe on an oblong, wooden object.

"Ah thought the room was full of coffins," Billy said to me later when we were safely at our own door. It was actually sideboards – we could see when our eyes adjusted to the dark – wardrobes and tables of various sizes. "Mostly sideboards," Billy said, there was at least ten of them. I bet that's where he keeps the stuff he steals or smuggles. He would likely have killed us and put us in them, if he had caught us."

All I knew was that I was black and blue, climbing over sharp-edged obstacles to reach the window, through which we escaped, and I was sure, another minute and I would have peed myself.

"Lucky they live in the close and not up the stairs," May said when we told her what had happened. She had been allowed to stay, sitting by the fire with wee Jay and had been introduced to Jack Easton as John Wallace's wife.

"He just nodded to me and told her tae get his tea. I don't know what a' the carry on was about. He was drunk right enough.

He fell asleep wi' his head on that lovely big sponge cake," she told us. "You know, the one wi' the lemon curd in it."

We never found out the answer to the mystery of Mrs Freckle's man. He was probably just another wee Glesca bloke who became a ten feet high ogre when he had too much of the national drink inside him, but we preferred to think of him as a smuggler and potential murderer. Mrs Freckle's only comment was, "He likes the place tae oorsels at teatime. Ah didnae expect him back sae early," but she never had us back again.

There was more excitement to talk about soon. It was just as well that Mammy had not handed over her Family Allowance book for that loan, because a man up the street was arrested for illegal money-lending and there was a queue outside the police station, of women, claiming their books back from dozens found in his possession. Mammy was quite smug about it, "Daft bitches!" she scorned. "They should never have let him have their books. What a showing up!"

After the man's arrest, we heard about a few 'beatings-up' and broken legs happening in and around the Wine Alley, but, to our disappointment, Mrs Freckle was not dragged from her bed and beaten up, or even arrested.

"Maybe she was just talking big," Vicky said. "She probably didn't really have anything to do with the money-lending, or the police would have arrested her, wouldn't they?"

Billy asked Robert Hood about the sideboards in the room, but he just laughed and said, "Whit dae ye mean? Everybody's got furniture in their rooms, haven't they? Except really poor, scruffy people." Not wanting to appear 'scruffy' (We only had one sideboard between three rooms) Billy left it at that, but continued to imagine bodies rotting there, or the loot from burglaries being stored there.

We loved reading and nobody ever censored what we read, apart from a prune-faced woman in the library, who used to look at the two books we had chosen apiece, every Saturday and say, "Far too old for you. Choose something from the children's shelves." We got round this by letting her stamp things like 'Anne of Green Gables' or 'Billy Bunter and The Big Top' while sneaking out 'Tales of Mystery and Imagination' by Edgar Alan Poe (Billy) and anything by Dickens for me. We didn't keep them but sneaked them back onto the shelves when 'prune-face' was busy with her vicious date-stamp, which she used like a lethal weapon, as if the books were blue-bottles to be squashed before they could do any damage.

It was Billy's love of Edgar Alan Poe and horror comics which gave us our fascination with violent death and rotting corpses. Whatever it was, we saw spectres and murderers all around us. There were plenty of 'mysteries' walking around Govan to feed our gory imaginations, and the Wine Alley was home to a fair whack of them.

Vicky

CHAPTER THREE

VICKY'S STORY

My Foolish Heart

I was happy when Daddy came back, although I didn't care for his hugging and kissing – it made me cringe. Mammy and I never got on. She said I was lazy because I hated housework and looking after my wee brother and sister and she said I was always putting on my cough just to get out of going to that dirty, wee village school, where the teachers all hated me and the other weans were common as muck and twice as thick. Well I was left now and, if I had my way, would soon be leaving home. My first job hadn't lasted long, but there would be others.

I remember how angry Daddy was when he found out about my job. "A servant!" he said. "A skivvy to some rich bitch! I'm not putting up wi' that. You want to learn something from your work and I don't mean how to say 'yes ma'am, no ma'am, anything you say ma'am'. And you sleep in the same room as the dog? Jesus Christ May! Why did you let her take a job like that?"

"There's nothing else for lasses about here. Anyway, she's given it up. She only stayed one day." Mammy answered. She was mad at me for telling him about the job. I hadn't meant to get her into trouble, but I thought it was only right that he should know. He asked me what I was working at and I told him about it.

It was the local minister who had put us on to it. The woman had seemed that nice when Mammy and I went to her house for the interview for the job – praising me up, saying how well-spoken I was and promising that I would be 'treated just like one of the family'. I was to look after her two under-fives and generally help with the housework. I had to live in (in my own room) and get one day a week off to go home. I was really excited about starting work.

Everything was different when I reported for my first day. She said my hair was untidy and I had to cover it with a horrible white cap, like Mammy's jelly bag and she made me cut my nails right to the quick, although they were already short and spotlessly clean – I was always very particular about my nails. It used to make Mammy mad the way I was always filing and buffing them, but I had read in the Women's Illustrated Weekly, that Granny Ross sent to me, that you can tell a lady by her well-kept hands.

Then she showed me my room. It was a big cupboard, off the scullery, with a camp bed and a scabby old chest of drawers. There was no window, but that wasn't the worst of it: taking up most of the floor space, was a dog's basket, filled by a mangy bundle of dirty brown fur, imitating a dog and smelling like stale dog's mess.

"Glen will keep you company," she smirked. "He's a good watchdog. He barks if anyone comes into the garden, but he's really friendly." The ugly thing was showing me its yellow teeth and I could picture them sunk into my leg and I could see the fleas doing a jig around his ears.

"I'm not staying here," I said. "You told me I would have a room of my own."

That had been the main attraction of the job: to get away from sleeping three in a bed with my two sisters, and my three brothers in another bed in the same room. I had already been planning things I would buy for my room off my pay – a vase for flowers and a vanity set (I wasn't sure what that was but I'd read that ladies had them on their dressing tables) and I had some nice flower pictures I had cut out of books. This room had nothing resembling a dressing table and it smelt of dog and dampness instead of the pot-pourri I had imagined.

She really could not see why a girl from a poor family objected to sharing a room with a dog. I could see by the puzzled look on her thin, parrotty face.

"Surely you are not homesick already," she tittered. "It will be nice for you to have a little room of your own surely, and Glen will be company for you. You don't have a dog at home do you? I would imagine your mother had enough to feed with all those brothers and sisters." She made my brothers and sisters seem like a shameful disease, which I should be glad to get rid of, and although I hated the way we all had to crowd into the one room to sleep and mealtimes reminded me of feeding time in the hen run at the farm along the road, I still preferred them to sleeping with a dog.

"I'm not sleeping in here with that thing!" I actually shouted at her although I knew ladies never raised their voices.

"Maybe you would like the guest room," she said sarcastically. "You are here to work as a servant you know, girl." I felt like poking her skelly eyes out and tearing at her scraggy, faded hair, but I thought the dog might go for me if I attacked her, so I just turned and walked out of 'my own little room' and started up the stairs out of the kitchen, with her running after me, twittering. "Come here girl. You will do as you're told (no wonder she needed someone to look after her weans. I bet they never did what she told them).

Mammy had given me a shilling, to last me until I got my wages from the bitch, but it was not enough for the bus fare right home. I took it as far as I could and walked the rest – about three miles. That didn't bother me that much. We were used to walking during our evacuation to the country and I was just glad to get away from that house.

"There's no daughter of mine going to be anybody's servant," Daddy raged at Mammy. "She wants a job wi' a future to it no' just fillin' the time till some country yokel marries her and gives her a squad of weans." My face was scarlet by this time and I was sorry I'd let slip about the job.

"If she's goin' to be serving people, she's better learning a trade while she's about it. There's plenty of hotel jobs going and her and Nancy can work together and look after each other. I'll talk to that fella that has the hotel in Ballantrae. He'll take them on. His brother was a Seaforth like me."

That was it. He was determined that none of us would go into service, yet Mammy was right, that was the only kind of work in the country for a young girl who had left school at fourteen.

The way he saw it, the hotel trade was different from service in a private house. It was a 'real' job, with prospects. Nancy and I loved working in the hotel. We did everything from serving in the dining room to bathing the owner's weans, but it was a laugh and the men that came in gave us loads of tips. That was what made him take us out of the job after just a couple of months – he didn't like the attention we were getting from the men. It was daft, because we knew how to look after oursels, but he didn't believe it.

There was only one way out of it, according to him – send us to stay with my Granny Ross in Glasgow, our home town before the war had uprooted us to the country. He took us to visit her and they had a long talk, which resulted in us really getting a room to ourselves and a job where we would learn a trade – fur-finishing in one of the biggest furriers in Glasgow.

At that time, every well-known woman owned a fur coat, or a stole – maybe even both. People hadn't started thinking about the horrible events that led up to the gorgeous mink or fox fur slung across the shoulders of the upper-classes and envied by those beneath them.

I wanted to stay in Granny Ross's house forever. It was the bottom house in a red-sandstone tenement building, with two bedrooms, a lovely big living room with a bay window, a kitchen and a real bathroom, that always had soft toilet roll and pink soap and towels that you couldn't see through. Granny told us she wanted us to take a bath at least twice a week and she would do our washing but we must help with the ironing and keep our own room tidy. These things were not duties to me, they were part of the life I had read about and thought I would never have.

Our house (it wasn't ours, we had been billeted there by the authorities at the time of the evacuation, and stayed on because we were homeless) always smelt like bleach, beef dripping and dirty bodies. Granny's smelt of Mansion polish and homemade soup. Our beds didn't have real sheets. They had rough ticking on the bottom and rough blankets next to your skin that made you itch. Granny's beds had lovely, smooth, linen sheets underneath and on top of your body: the blankets were fine white wool) Ayrshire blankets, Granny told me) and on top of everything was a patchwork quilt that made me think of Joseph's coat of many colours.

It was about seven o'clock when Daddy left to get his train. Wee Granda Ross, who was only about five feet and bow-legged, shook hands with him and wished him 'all the best', but Granny just gave a nod, as if she was shaking something off the end of her nose, which she was forever wiping, and said, "The lasses will be fine here. Their Aunty Jean's got them jobs, and we will see that they're looked after."

As soon as he was away, she said to me, "Right lassie, into the bath with you, and mind, wash your hair." I felt a bit hurt as if she thought I was dirty or something, but I was looking forward to getting into that slippery, white bath and using the pink soap, so I rinsed off the hurt with the big, yellow, squishy sponge that sat beside the soap dish.

When I got out of the bath and rubbed myself with the sweet smelling towels, while Nancy jumped in, she put her head round the door. "I got you a couple of nightgowns," she said, putting two pale blue, long sleeved gowns, trimmed with lace on the neck and sleeves, on the towel rail. I had never owned a nightgown – not that I could remember anyway – and wearing it as I sat by the fire, drinking cocoa and eating biscuits, with my grandparents, I suddenly felt like a wee girl: like the baby in the family, who would be looked after and petted. Wee Granda switched on the radio and the four of us sat there listening to a play, until she noticed I was nodding and sent us to bed.

That was the perfect time in my life, even though Nancy sometimes got on my nerves. She used to say, "I wonder how Conn and Roddy are getting on and if Mammy misses us?" but I never thought about any of the family. I'd had to think of them all the time I was growing up; being the eldest and now I just wanted to be a person, not a big sister. They belonged to a world of dirty necks, scabby knees and snotty noses. We were like toffs now, with clean underwear every day and handbags and gloves. I tried to speak proper, particularly when there were any customers about. I could kill Nancy for making faces at me behind their backs, but sometimes I had to hide my face in my sewing to keep from laughing.

Olswang and Plottle's was the name of the furriers where we were learning to be fur-finishers and maybe cutters or machinists, if we were good enough. Usually the cutters were men. There were only two in our place and they didn't speak much to us. We were just silly wee lasses to them, but I made a point of being polite to them and admiring their work, just in case I got a chance to learn their skills.

At first I felt a bit creepy about working with fur, thinking of it as dead animals, but when I saw the beautiful coats and things it could be made into, I began to enjoy working with it and it was interesting when customers came in for a fitting of a made-to-measure garment or just select something from our window display. I wanted to be like these women, oh I don't mean in looks: they were mostly fat and you felt that there was another smell beneath their expensive perfume, not so nice.

It was the expensive I wanted, expensive shoes, expensive coats and hats, expensive kid gloves, even expensive handkerchiefs (which I had always called hankies before).

I started to save up from my wages, which Granny let us keep, so that I could dress like a lady – instead of buying a cheap blouse or make-up every week, the way Nancy did. Sometimes I pictured myself coming in as a rich wife and talking to the girls as they bent over their sewing, while I was fitted for a full length mink or one of the little silver fox capes I often tried on when Chrissie, the forewoman, was out.

I liked when the customers spoke to me, although they were a bit snobbish and nosey at times, asking questions like, "And where do you live, miss?" or "Do you come from a big family?" or "What made you take up this kind of work?" Sometimes, if their men were with them they would lean over and whisper stupid things about boyfriends and whether I would like a fur coat, but I just smiled as if they were being really clever.

I never told them that I came from a big family, not because I was ashamed. I felt they would feel sorry for me and think I must be lower class if I did. High class people did not have big families, not even Catholics. No, I told them that Nancy and I usually lived in the country with our parents, but a friend of our aunt had asked us to come and work for her, so we had come to live with our grandmother, who we helped out. I don't suppose they believed me, even if they bothered to listen to my answers to their questions. Nancy did not back me up in my lies, she just nodded or shook her head when they asked her questions, so they stopped bothering with her at all – they probably thought she was shy, or just stupid.

One of the hundreds of things I loved about staying with Granny Ross was that she was always standing with the door open when we got in from work at night and we could tell what was for dinner by the smell wafting down the close. Friday nights were my favourites, because sometimes, after we had eaten, the three of us, Granny, Nancy and me would go to the pictures.

One Friday it was different.

She was standing in her usual place and the smell of the ham soup started our juices flowing as soon as we got in the close, but she wasn't smiling. In fact her thin lips and red cheeks made me wonder if we had done something to make her angry. I hoped Nancy hadn't left the bathroom in a mess that morning. She was not always as tidy as me.

"You've got a visitor," she said, turning and walking in front of us into the living room.

It was Daddy. He stood up and put his arms round the two of us and I knew he'd had a couple of pints, although he wasn't drunk. I always liked his smell – tobacco, brilliantine and alcohol, but somehow, this time, it made me kind of scared. I felt I was not going to like his reason for being there. Before he even spoke I was saying to myself, "I'm not leaving here. I'm not going back."

"What a pair o' wee smashers!" he said, ruffling our hair and squeezing the life out of us. "What have you been feeding then Granny? I would hardly have recognised them. Well are you pleased to see your wee Daddy? Just wait 'til you hear what I've got to tell you.

"Let them settle down and get their dinner first," Granny said with ice cracking in her voice.

"We're all moving back to Glasgow. We've got a house." He said after we had eaten and helped Granny clear up. I felt Granny's boiled ham and potatoes swirling around in my stomach as if it was about to come back up. I didn't want to go back to staying with my brothers and sisters: putting up with them touching my things; smelly nappies and snottery noses. This was how I wanted to live, where there was privacy and the clean smell of polish and you didn't have to listen to loud chewing and slurping at meal times, and the sheets on the bed were clean every week. I didn't want to go back.

Nancy made me mad by saying. "That's great Daddy. I've missed Mammy and the weans, even Billy and Maggie. When can we see the house?" I could have choked her. Didn't she know she was hurting Granny's feelings? I didn't want to see the stupid house and I hadn't missed any of them. This was how I wanted to live.

"I want to stay here," I said. "There'll be more room if I stay here, won't there?"

"Oh, there's plenty of room – it's a five apartment, that means three big bedrooms, a living room, kitchenette and bathroom, and I've ordered some new furniture. You two will be first to see it. I'll pick you up tomorrow morning early."

"I want to stay here with my granny." I knew I sounded whingey and sulky but I was desperate.

"She could stay here," wee Granda put in. "We like having both of them here, and it would give you more room, right enough."

"No, she's going to stay with her family. I don't want anyone else bringing up my weans. I've seen too much of that. It always causes problems. Anyway her Mammy needs all the help she can get in a big house like that, and looking after seven weans.

He leaned over and patted my knee. "You'll like the new place hen and you can visit your granny any time and even bring some of the rest of them with you – eh Granny?"

Nancy and I had a real fight that night. She said that I had hurt Daddy's feelings and I nipped her arm really hard and told her she was a thoughtless bitch for hurting Granny's feelings. She said I was a snob and thought I was better than my own family. I had the last word by saying that I was certainly better than a fat red-haired keelie like her, before Granny knocked on the door and said it was time we were sleeping.

*

The close at number 16 Kellas Street was clean enough, but the walls were painted cream at the top half and a horrible, dingy, wine colour at the bottom. They didn't have tiles like Granny's close and there was a smell of cats. Only one room in the house had been papered in an unnatural looking rose pattern. The rest were covered in yellow distemper, the colour of wee Jay's nappy contents. The kitchenette was half the size of Granny's and smelt like stale bread.

We chose the middle bedroom, leading off the lobby, as it had a gas fire and Daddy had bought us a second-hand chest of drawers to keep our stuff in. In Granny's we had had a wardrobe, a tallboy, a dressing table and two pink basket chairs. Still I decided not to show how miserable I was and joined in the fun as we helped Daddy to clean the place ready for the arrival of Mammy and the rest of them. Then he took us out for a fish tea in quite a posh place, which cheered me up a lot, although Nancy kept forgetting and lifting her chips with her fingers.

The people in the close were really lower class, apart from maybe the Cuthills on the bottom right. They seemed quite respectable. Every time Nancy and I went out or came in there would be some scruffy looking boy or man whistling at us and saying things like 'Hello gorgeous' or 'How about a wee kiss hen?'. The crowd of layabouts that stood at the corner of the street started calling Nancy 'Ginger' but she just laughed and kind of swaggered when she passed them. I never looked at the road they were on.

There was one lad in particular who really made me shudder. He lived across the landing from us. Terry was his name; everyone called him Big Terry, I just couldn't stand him or his wee bow-legged sisters, who were always trying to be friendly to me when we met in the close. Roddy and Conn called them the 'cowgirls', which was really cruel, as it wasn't their fault they had rickets – a lot of lower class people did, especially Catholics (Granny Ross told me).

Daddy told us to have nothing to do with the blokes who lived in the Wine Alley (I hated that name). He said we would move away from there once we could get a house in a better area. He said there were too many Catholics around for his liking.

*

The night he told us that he was going back in the army, I felt he didn't care what happened to us, although he said he was doing it for our good, so that there would be more money coming in and it would only be for a couple of years. I still liked my work in Olswang and Plottle's, although working with the furs made me cough a lot.

Every night when we went to bed, I thought how different it was from Granny's and thought of ways I could get back there, or at least out of Kellas Street. There was only one bed in our room and Nancy and I slept at one end and Maggie the other. I didn't mind Nancy but Maggie hardly ever had a bath and her feet smelt like rotten cheese, right in our noses, so I suggested that she should sleep crossways, but that meant we couldn't stretch our legs out. So it was either put up with the smell or get cramp from lying with our legs bent. Sometimes I gave her a good kick just because I was fed up with her being there. Nancy told me not to be cruel, that it wasn't her fault. Nothing seemed to annoy Nancy.

Things got better in some ways after Daddy left. Maggie moved into sleep on a folding bed-chair in the living room and we got our room to ourselves, and Mammy, more or less, let us come and go as we pleased, where Daddy had always wanted to know who we were out with and nagged us to help with the housework. What got worse was that she let the boys and Maggie do what they liked as well and they got totally out of hand, and another thing – she started sitting at the close with all these horrible, fat, common women.

Big Terry sometimes stood and gave the women his patter (you would have thought he was a film star the way the giggled and laughed at him, like wee girls) and he took my arm one night when I was walking in the close and said, "When is the best looking lassie in Govan gonnae go out wi' me then?"

My face went scarlet, I could feel the heat of it and the horrible women screeched like banshees, but I just shook off his arm and walked on up the stair without answering. I heard one of the women – I thought it was Mrs Ranachan – saying, "Snooty wee bitch."

I was glad I was snooty and not common like them. Granny had said to us, "It's up to you to keep up your standards. Remember you're better than these people and don't have anything to do with them." I knew she was right.

For ages after I was in the house and sitting reading my library book (I made myself read a book a week) I felt as if his fingers were still holding my arm. I looked when I stripped for bed and there were three blue lines like a snake bracelet, just above my elbow. For the rest of that week it was as if I had tied a piece of string around a finger to remind myself of something. He kept coming into my mind. Worst of all, I dreamt about him, and Nancy pretended that I had said his name in my sleep.

"Surely you haven't got a notion for him?" she said. "He's like Joe Palooka AND he's a catholic. Daddy would kill you!"

There was one of the cutters at work who was always asking me out. He came from a good family and was really well-spoken and not bad looking. The other girls were always telling me he was a really good catch, but he made me want to be cruel to him, the way he tried to please me – always giving me the best work and helping me tidy my bench, even bringing in cakes for my morning tea. It made me cringe and his white, tapering hands gave me the creeps. I thought of a vampire when I looked at them. I finally gave in and went to the pictures with him, he treated me like a lady, buying chocolates and an ice at the interval and holding my hand during the film – not even squeezing it, just holding it as if he thought it would break. When he walked me to the subway he told me all about his home in Bearsden (That's where I wanted to live), where he lived with his parents and his two sisters, and how he would like me to meet them some day. All I could think about was how we could get over the obstacle of his great hooked nose if he tried to kiss me on the lips. He didn't. He held my face and kissed me on the forehead and I felt that everyone on the subway could see the wet mark it must have left. As I sat, staring at my reflection in the window opposite, I had a sudden picture of me walking with him through the line-up of women at the close and I gave the drunk opposite me the wrong idea by grinning like an idiot, making him think his night was just beginning.

I knew that I had to find another way out of Wine Alley. The cutter was not the answer.

Everyone took turns in giving parties at their houses. We had been to all the other girls' houses and Nancy said it was our turn or they would think there was something wrong with our house. All we had to do was ask Mammy and that would not be hard.

"We'll get the cakes and things," Nancy coaxed. "All you'll have to do is keep the weans out of the road. Conn and Roddy go out on a Saturday night anyway. What do you think Mammy?"

The party was the start of me going with Terry – my way out of the Wine Alley.

"You're not going to ask *him* are you?" nosey Maggie shrieked, reading the list I was making. I shoved her head off my shoulder, thinking I better watch my head for nits from her. She was always clawing, like a dog with fleas.

"Mind your own business. You won't be here anyway," I shouted at her.

"Let me see," Nancy held her hand out. "Remember it's my party too. Who's wee Nosey Parker talking about? Not Captain Hook from the cutting room?" She looked down the list, nodding at every name until she came to the last one. I had written Terry Watson.

"You can't ask him! I don't mind his young sister, but not him. He's mingin' and we don't even know him!" I took the list back and scored out the name.

"OK then," I said. "It was only because we don't have enough men, and he does live next door. Mammy said if we ask some of the neighbours they won't make such a fuss about the noise. I'll just ask Captain Hook as you call him. That will make numbers even, OK?"

"You better ask Big Terry then, maybe he'll be all right. He couldn't be as smarmy as Captain Hook, but I'm not goin' out wi' him at postman's knock, no matter what." I added his name back on the list and forced myself not to go red. I knew if I did Nancy would imagine all sorts of things. She thought everybody was like her – fancying everything in trousers.

The day of the party, we were working in the morning until twelve o'clock. I wanted to get home and get organised but of course Nancy had to buy something to wear – my clothes were already laid out on our bed. She settled on a pale green, sweetheart neck blouse, which I had to admit she suited, in a flashy kind of way. I was wearing a silver-grey chiffon blouse with a Peter Pan collar and bishop sleeves with a grey, gabardine, straight skirt.

When we finally did get in, we went absolutely cleaning mad. Things that had never been scrubbed were scrubbed white; things that had never felt a touch of polish were polished until our faces shone back at us; even wee Jay was put into the big sink and had the ingrained dirt scrubbed from his knees until they came up red raw. I don't know how many times I slapped Maggie's and Billy for getting in the road. I finally gave them sixpence each to go buy sweets and warned them not to come back 'till dinner time, which they were to eat in the kitchenette.

The food – cakes and sandwiches – and the drink, ginger beer, cola and Irn Bru – was laid out on a cloth on top of the big, old-fashioned sideboard that Granny Ross had given Mammy. It looked quite classy. A bit like the buffets rich people have, I thought in my ignorance.

Subways was a game people would laugh at now but it seemed really daring to us. I can't remember the exact rules, just that it involved people having the names of subway stations in Glasgow and when your station was called out you had to kiss the person with the same station name. The lights went out during the kissing and when they came back on, everybody had to move one place in the circle. It sounds a bit pointless, but it gave us the chance to kiss every other member of the opposite sex.

Terry found out my station name and managed to always end up kissing me and when the lights went on there was a lot of jealous remarks about cheating. I knew a few of the other lads wanted to 'get off' with me, but I didn't care what they thought, I couldn't think of anything else but the hard way he held me on his knee and the way my lips felt, as if a cold sore was starting from his rough kissing. Nancy threw me a few dirty looks but I didn't let on I saw her. The party was much better than I thought it would be.

He did the same thing at postman's knock. He asked me my number and told me his so that we could keep asking for one another to come out into the hall for the number of kisses requested. Nancy spoilt this by making me change my number with one of the girls from our work and giving Terry a new number too. I thought she was just jealous because the chap she fancied had got off with someone else. I told her that when we eventually got to bed in the early hours of the morning.

Terry was the last to leave and he and I stood talking on the landing until Mammy came out and told me to go to bed. She didn't look very pleased, but I supposed at the time this was because it was really late and the house was getting cold with me having the door open. Nancy told me later what was really making her angry.

"The Watsons are Catholics," she whispered. "Mammy hates Catholics, so does Granny Ross. She'll go mad if she finds out your goin' out wi' one."

"Who says I'm going out with him?" I whispered back. I was really hurt that he hadn't asked me to go out yet and I didn't want Maggie to find out about it. The nosey wee nuisance.

The next night I watched for him coming in the close and then went and stood at our door waiting for him to reach the landing. (Mammy kept shouting, asking me what I was doing but I never let on I heard). I whispered his name before he had time to put his key in the lock and he came over and pushed me into the lobby, outside the bathroom door. He kissed me so hard I thought my head was going through the wall. The grip of his hands, on my arms, dug into the bruises he had already made there and I had to hold my breath to keep from squealing, but I knew he didn't mean to hurt me. He just didn't know his own strength. I would explain to him how easily I bruised and he would be more gentle in future. We must have stood there for about ten minutes before he let me breathe, but when he did I said, "There's a great picture on at the Vogue. Do you want to go on Saturday?"

"Aye," he answered. "But I don't have much money, so it'll be the cheap seats."

"That doesn't matter." I tried not to show him how pleased I was in case he thought I was desperate.

"I'll give your door a knock about seven then," he said as he went to his own door. I only had time to nod before Billy pushed passed to get into the bathroom. I was so sick of wee brothers and sisters! I felt really self-conscious walking out the close with him, but quite proud. He was wearing a shirt and tie, and a suit, which was a bit shabby but he had made an effort I thought. I was wearing my red woollen coat over a black pencil skirt and my grey poplin blouse. I knew I looked really classy and I didn't even turn around when the old witches at the close got in a few digs as we passed. Terry had walked in front of me down the stairs but I caught up with him in the close and took his arm, just like any other winching couple. This is what caused the remarks. That old biddy Ranachan said we made a 'good looking couple' and somebody else said, "Big Terry's got hisself a girlfriend." And they all laughed as if something witty and clever had been said. I thought he was going to stop and speak to them for a minute, so I squeezed his arm and pushed past them.

After that night, people accepted that we were winching. We didn't have a lot of dates because Terry had no job, but he came and stood with me every night in our little corner by the bathroom door. We never did more than kiss, although he sometimes tried to force my legs apart with his knee or slip his hand inside my blouse. It wasn't easy for him but he understood that I was not the kind of girl that did anything before she was married.

It was his sister, Bridget, who put it into my head to become a Roman Catholic. She said that nobody in their family would ever get their mother's blessing for a mixed marriage. I didn't care about giving up being a protestant. I had always been brought up to think of Catholics as being workshy, having big families and not having much of an education, but everybody in Terry's family worked – apart from Terry, but that was just temporary bad luck – and although they were quite a big family and not all that bright, they were always clean and tidy and very friendly to me.

Bridget went with me the first time I went to the convent for instructions and she bought me a beautiful ivory prayer book. Jinty gave me a string of really nice rosary beads. I had a feeling I was going to enjoy learning about being a catholic and 'being welcomed into the Holy Church', as the priest put it. He was the spitting image of Barry Fitzgerald, playing a priest, and had a lovely Irish accent. (Far better than the minister who had visited us when we first moved in to number 16. He looked like death warmed up and spoke with a bool in his mouth). It seemed to be a much more romantic religion, with lovely pictures and more drama somehow.

I didn't tell anyone what I was doing. I decided to wait until I was actually a catholic and they couldn't do anything about it, but I was dying to get married in the chapel and thought of nothing else.

Mammy spoiled it all.

*

It was that wee bitch, Maggie, who started it. She was noseying in my drawer and brought her wee, smelly pal in to see the prayer book and the rosary. Mammy caught them and went off her head. I've never seen anything like it. I never thought I could feel so ashamed or hate anyone so much.

In front of the whole family, she burnt them! I saw her give a little jump and rub her leg when one of the beads, that were shooting out of the fire like peas out of a shooter, must have hit her. I wished it was a bullet through her heart. The flames, that melted the picture of Our Lady and Baby Jesus, were the shade of green I imagined emeralds to be. I thought of the picture in my school history book, of Joan of Arc being burnt at the stake and I could feel the heat making my face burn and my eyes water.

Everybody was absolutely silent, for a change, after Mammy had said her disgusting speech. Maggie was first to rush from the room. I could see that she was crying but I was determined I wouldn't cry for any of them.

She knew that I had told Daddy I wanted to marry Terry. She read his answer out to the whole family. He promised me a big, white wedding, with all the trimmings, if I would just wait until he came home, but I couldn't. Terry was the man I wanted to marry and I was not going to risk losing him by keeping him hanging on. Besides I wanted a nice place of my own – like Granny Ross's.

"We'll get married in the registry office," I told him a couple of nights after the burning of the prayer book. "And later on, when things have settled down, we can get married in the chapel. She can't stop me becoming a Catholic when I'm a married woman."

So that was it settled. I got myself a lovely, pale blue, two-piece, with a hat to match and Terry a grey pinstriped suit (I didn't tell anyone I'd paid for his suit). Nancy was my bridesmaid.

She had joined the WRAF by then and was home on her first leave, so she wore her uniform. Conn was best man and he was wearing his very first suit. I remember it as a good wedding. Nancy and I kept getting the giggles, seeing our wee brother dressed up like a man and she tried to talk Terry into going for a drink. He said he had never drunk and never would – I felt really proud of him for that – but he took us for a fish tea. Then the four of us went to the pictures in Green's Playhouse (it was Glenn Ford and Rita Hayworth in *Gilda*) and Terry and I left before the end of the picture to go to the room in his auntie's house for our first night. I wished we could have booked an hotel, but he said that was a waste of money.

I have never told anyone about that night, and I never will.

Mammy had calmed down a bit now that I wasn't becoming a catholic, so she let us have the middle room until we got a place. When we did get it, it was a room in one of the big, posh houses near Paisley Road. It was quite near where Granny Ross stayed but she wasn't very keen on Terry, so I did not see much of her.

Still I had a husband and a place of my own, away from the Wine Alley.

Life might be OK after all.

CHAPTER FOUR

NANCY

My Nanny with the laughing face

I've never been good at making my face say different from what I feel and much as I tried to appear as upset as Vicky when Daddy told us we were leaving Granny Ross's to live with the rest of the family in the house in Kellas Street – I tried to look sad to be leaving. I didn't want to hurt Granny Ross – I could feel my mouth shaping into a smile. I had really missed all of them, particularly Conn and Roddy and the new baby, wee Jay. I couldn't help saying, "That's great Daddy, I've missed everybody, even Billy and Maggie." Vicky looked daggers at me.

It had been fine staying with Granny and wee Granda, but a bit like always having to be on your Sunday best behaviour. Granny was a great cook and I had never been in such a clean house. The smell of Mansion polish takes me right back there whenever I smell it. The thing was, I was only fifteen, in my first job and wanting to spread my wings a bit. Instead I felt we were like two Sunday school teachers the way we lived and even dressed. Granny nearly had an Annie Rooney when I bought a burnt sienna lipstick (orange) and put a thin smear of it on when she was taking us on our weekly trip to the pictures. My emerald green chiffon scarf made her face go purple.

"Take a leaf from your sister's book," she said. "Dress like a lady at all times and you'll be treated like a lady. Showy girls attract the wrong kind of attention from men. Remember that!"

She had bought us leather gloves, sensible shoes and lisle stockings, which we not only wore for work but on nights out as well. Most of the other young girls in Olswang and Plottle's wore bare legs and wedge-heeled shoes with peep-toes. Vicky and I were much better looking than any of them, but we looked like a pair of old maids. Vicky didn't mind. She suited the ladylike look. I hated it, but I couldn't affront Granny by showing myself in my true colours.

I felt like scratching her eyes out when she told Daddy that she wanted to stay with Granny and included me in it, and when wee Granda said it would be all right, I felt like kicking his wee legs from under him. I wanted to say it wouldn't be all right for me but Daddy saved me the bother when he said, "No, they're going to stay with their family, I don't want anyone else bringing up my weans. I've seen too much of that. It always causes problems." He said that Mammy needed us to help because it was a big house we were moving in to and when he patted her knee and told her she would really like the place and could visit Granny any time, I wanted to yell at her to at least try to look pleased, but she didn't. She just started clearing the table, managing to hold her body that way she had of letting people know that she didn't want anything to do with them. I'd seen her doing it to the fellas at work that she didn't want anything to do with. I'd seen her doing it to the fellas on the subway too. She even did it to me sometimes, so I was used to it but I could see Daddy wasn't and he looked cut to the bone.

We had a big fight when we went to bed that night. She said I was a cruel red-haired bitch for hurting Granny and wee Granda's feelings and nipped me so hard I thought her nails must have met through my skin. I told her she was a goody goody snob for hurting Daddy's feelings and thinking she was better than her own family. I got the last word by saying she wouldn't be able to keep her nose in a book when she had to help with the housework, before Granny knocked on the door and said it was time we were sleeping – it was nine o'clock.

*

I knew as soon as we turned the corner into Kellas Street (Daddy laughed when he told us that some people called it The Wine Alley) and the corner boys whistled after us, that I was going to like this much better than Granny Ross's. Vicky's face was red and she held her head up as if she was watching something fascinating happening in the sky, but I gave them a smile and kind of swaggered as we passed them, the way I had seen Lana Turner doing in a picture. They went mad!

The house was not as fancy, or clean, as Granny's, but it was ok. Vicky and I were in the middle room, off the lobby. The worst thing was the bedclothes. In Granny's we had a huge double bed with linen sheets, fluffy white blankets and a satin quilt and bedspread to match. In our new house we didn't have a top sheet, or a quilt and the blankets were grey ones that Daddy had got through the army – and Maggie had to sleep with us.

She was more of a wee oddity than ever, but I liked her. Her and I had a laugh, especially when Vicky was telling us off or moaning about Maggie stealing her knickers. I felt sorry for her, she was so skinny and Mammy made her wear cast-offs, that never fitted her. She told me about how she had got the whole class at school to get their own back on a wee clipe and I felt quite proud of her (although I thought she might be exaggerating a bit). Vicky made her sleep across the bottom of the bed so that she wouldn't be too close to us. She was a bit smelly and I had seen Mammy putting nit stuff in her hair, but it wasn't her fault. Even Vicky had had nits at one time, when we were evacuated, although she would never admit it.

A great thing about being back staying with Mammy and Daddy was that we were allowed to go to the dancing with our pals as long as we came in at a reasonable hour, and nobody said anything about my makeup. Vicky went a couple of times but she said the people that went were all scruffs and wee hairies, so I just went with my pals from work.

A lot of the girls went looking for a lumber, but I went for the dancing I loved. I couldn't get enough of the smell of Brylcreem, face powder and 'Evening in Paris' and the bright colours of the girl's blouses and skirts and the fella's white shirts and ties – they were not allowed in without a tie or if they smelled of beer – with the light and shadow of the glitter ball on the ceiling making them look as if they were underwater and the girls tortured permed hair like seaweed in the waves.

I know I've made it sound romantic, but it really was a magical place and to top it all there was music. I never wanted to stop dancing. I grudged the time between dances and if I was not lifted right away, I pulled one of my pals onto the dance floor and danced with her. That didn't happen very often. Usually two or three fellas made a bee-line to ask me up for each dance and I would pick the one that looked like the best dancer. Sometimes they asked you to stay up for the next dance but I seldom did that. It usually meant they were after more than a dance.

At home in number 16 everything was fine. I went to the pictures sometimes with Conn and Roddy, or I would clean

Maggie up and take her if they were out with their pals; Vicky and I got on ok, although her snobbish ways still drove me mad and she moaned if I happened to borrow any of her precious clothes. We were just so different. It couldn't be helped. She sneaked in with the fat toffs that came into Olswang and Plottle's and watched us working on their fur coats as if we were some strange thing in a bottle. I either ignored them or insulted them, when I knew I could get away with it.

"Why do you suck up to these sweaty, ugly toads?" I used to say and she would look down her turned up nose and say:

"Some of us want to better ourselves you know."

We were only in the new house about a year when Daddy told us he was going back into the army. I didn't know what to think. Part of me understood that he was probably bored with his job in the gasworks after all the excitement of the war, and disappointed that life hadn't turned out the way he dreamt about when he was a prisoner, yet I felt that he was a bit unfair to Mammy, after all, she had coped with us on her own while he was away and had another baby just nine months after he was back. Surely she deserved her life to be a bit better too? He had seemed really happy when he first came back – all proud of his big, grown up sons and daughters – always teaching us card games and telling us how we should try to 'better' ourselves and get out of the 'Wine Alley' as soon as we could. I don't know what happened but suddenly he stayed out drinking more – hardly spoke to us and we could hear him and Mammy arguing at night, although we couldn't make out what they were saying. Sometimes Mammy's eyes were all red in the morning.

Another thing, I don't think Vicky would have got in tow with Big Terry, if he had stayed at home.

It was funny how everything began to change for us around that time. Because Daddy went away, we were allowed to have a party and that's when Vicky met Big Terry – well not the first time she had met him – he lived next door – but the first time she had any contact with him.

He must have had his eye on her before that night because he put whoever was calling the numbers at Postman's Knock or Subways, up to always calling their two numbers together and kept her outside for ages. She told me later that she had given a different number to the 'postman' when she was out and said only one letter, but he had called Terry's number and said twelve letters (which meant twelve kisses). At first I thought she would snub him and refuse to go outside when it was obviously set up – but she didn't. Her face got really flushed and I had never seen her hair so untidy, or her blouse sticking out from the waistband of her skirt. She just did not seem like our Vicky – the lady.

It was quite late – Mammy had been in twice and told us it was time everyone went home – when I struggled from under a lad who seemed to be trying to eat the face off me and noticed that Vicky and Big Terry had disappeared. They were standing winching in the lobby when I was showing the rest of the crowd the door. I cannot think of anything that had ever surprised me more! Our high-minded sister, Vicky, snuggling up to that big, scruffy lout, and him a catholic as well! Mammy would have a fit and God knows what Daddy would do if he ever found out!

She started going out with him after that, although they seemed to spend most of their dates in our lobby, just outside the lavatory door, so that we had to squeeze past to get a pee!

*

It was just after the party when I first saw the advertisement.

Rita, my best pal at work, and I were reading our horoscopes during the tea break and it was at the bottom of the page. It was the picture of a girl in uniform with a handsome RAF officer smiling in the background that made me look twice. The writing under the picture said that joining the Women's Royal Air Force meant that you would 'Have a useful career and see the world'. That wasn't the exact words but it was what it meant. There was a cut out form attached to send away for more details, so I filled it in, stole an envelope from the office and posted it on the way home from work.

I wanted to do something different from what every girl I knew seemed to want. Find a boyfriend, get engaged, save up for a big white wedding, get married, give up work and have weans. I knew Mammy had got married when she was seventeen and she have never done anything else but look after us – apart from a job in a baker's shop after she left school, where Daddy had met her. I was going to do a lot of other things before I settled to married life and weans. Maybe the WRAF was the way to do it. Besides I had just seen Ann Sheridan in a film where she wore a uniform, with her red hair in a roll below her peaked cap. She looked just the way I wanted to look – for a while anyway.

The only people I told were Conn and Roddy, apart from Rita, who went all huffy because she was too young to join. They said it was a great idea and I would probably marry some pilot from a very rich family and I could take them to stay with me in his London mansion and they would become famous, for something or other.

Things at number 16 were awful at this time. Mammy had found Vicky's stuff for being converted to a Catholic and threw it all on the fire. It was a cruel, mad thing to do. I felt really sorry for

Vicky, but I couldn't tell her. It was as if she had a hard shell of ice around her and would not let anyone say a kind word to her or even speak to her at all. I knew her much better than Mammy did. The more anyone tried to stop her the more determined she would be to marry Big Terry.. It was a matter of pride now and pride was what drove her always.

So while my sister planned her wedding – which would have to be a registry office affair as she would not be allowed to get married in the Catholic church, being a protestant and his family would throw him out if he got married in a Protestant church – I wrote to Daddy, asking him to give his permission for me to join the WRAF.

Mammy just laughed when I eventually told her about my plans. I had been summoned to my first interview by then. "I thought it was only your sister that was mad – wanting to marry that big pape – but she seems to have infected you," she said. "What on Earth do you want to join up for?"

It wasn't that I hated my life as it was in the Wine Alley. It was a good enough life: I wanted to see what other places and lives were like. I hadn't really thought that much about *why* I was doing it. I just thought of myself as that girl in the advert: And the creepiness of sewing up dead animal skins was beginning to get to me. I felt sure that if the women who wore them had to handle them before we put silk linings in to cover the inside of their poor skins; or saw the shape of all the little bodies that go into one mink coat, they would not have been so keen to wear them.

Olswang and Plottle had taken up too much of my life. I wanted out.

Daddy gave his permission gladly, "I'm really proud that my wee girl is trying to make something of herself," he said in his letter. "It's a great life in the forces. Just remember to keep yourself decent among those RAF men – It's easy to get a bad name about yourself and not easy to live it down. I know I can trust you hen and you will make me even more proud."

So, I just had to pass the medical and I would be away.

Vicky lent me her white blouse with the rolled collar (I could borrow anything at that time as she was inside a wall of wedding plans and never heard what was said outside of it). I wore it with my green-checked suit, which had a belted jacket and breast pockets, so I thought it looked quite like a uniform. I tried to put my hair into a severe bun, but it had sprung out of the bobby pins by the time I came out of the close mouth, so I just left it as it was – like a rusty cloud round my head.

I saw Jinty Wilson – Terry's sister – in the queue for the tram. She waved to me and I had to go and stand beside her, although I hated that because she was so wee that I got a crick in my neck talking to her – even with her twelve inch platforms on. Still she was really quite a nice wee person, if only somebody would tell her that a brown tight skirt and a green feather and shell, hand knitted jumper had never been fashionable, even in our granny's day and never would be, and her swing-back jacket made her look like a candle snuffer.

"Where are you off to all brammed up?" she asked in a voice that made everybody in the queue turn to stare at me.

"I've got an interview for a job," I answered through my teeth. "Where are you going?"

She tossed her wee mousey head, "I've got an interview as well," she said. "I've applied to join the WRAF. I've got a medical today. I'm shaking in my shoes. Where's your interview?"

I couldn't stop myself from laughing in her face. Surely they did not take midgets in the forces!

"The same place," I said, suddenly feeling that I really liked her. There was no possibility that she would be accepted and I felt sorry for her in advance, but glad too that she would not be joining up like me.

The medical was a doddle for me and I came out with a bundle of papers about where and when I was to report for my initial training – which would take six weeks – I knew my hair was hanging like rat's tails by the time I came out and Vicky's blouse was damp with scared sweat, but I felt like turning cartwheels (I had never been able to do them before) while I waited for wee Jinty.

She came out looking smaller than ever, as though she had been stood on, and for once she was not smiling, "Poor wee soul," my good side thought, "I could have told you they wouldn't want a midget," my wee horned self answered. It was my good side that spoke.

"What a rotten shame," I said. "What did they say?" I was quite proud of not smirking.

She pulled herself up, thrusting out her green feather and shell bust and tossing her perm. "I was just what they wanted. I passed everything. In fact they said I am perfect, my height let me down, I'm only an inch too short. Have you ever heard anything so ridiculous?" I had never heard such a big lie, but the tears in her eyes stopped me from saying so.

"Come on," I said, pulling her arm through mine. "I'll buy you a coffee and a doughnut." (That was two of the things the yanks had left behind, along with chewing gum and a lot of wee bastard weans).

I nodded my head off in encouragement when she said, over and over again, that she would make herself grow that extra inch in no time and apply again – or she might apply for the NAAFI.

Height surely wouldn't matter there? She never mentioned about my sister going with her brother and I was glad of that. All I wanted to do was get home and tell everyone the good news, and write to Daddy and tell him.

"Who's going to help me keep this big house going now, with only your daddy's money coming in?" was all Mammy said, but I knew she was really quite proud of me. Conn and Roddy insisted on saluting me at every turn and Maggie asked me if I would have to get all my hair shaved off (I think she was confusing being in to the WRAF with entering a convent). Vicky actually smiled and said she would be glad to get her clothes to herself and Billy wanted to know if I would get my own aeroplane. Big Terry made his usual stupid remarks and kept calling me Biggles until I could have killed him.

Nothing could spoil it for me. I already felt much more grown up, away from home and everything it meant. I practised telling Chrissie, the forewoman, in front of the mirror, that I no longer needed her boring, disgusting job, that I was beginning a real career, but it didn't turn out like that.

When I walked into the workroom at Olswang and Plottle's, thinking it would be the last time its hairy dust would make me sneeze, I saw a circle of laughing, cheering faces and a space cleared on one of the benches for a plate of cakes and several small, fascinating parcels – Vicky had got the news to my workmates first and Chrissie had arranged a 'send-off'. My spiteful farewell speech seemed like the kind of thing a wee, daft lassie would say. I shoved it into the wastebasket of my mind. Instead, Chrissie made a speech wishing me well for the future and hoping that I would come back to see them all when I got my first leave. "Bring us back one of your handsome pilots," she said, blushing. "Don't keep them all to yourself."

*

The first leave was not long in coming. It arrived at the end of the best and worst six weeks of my life. It was worse than school for being shouted at and criticised and the cold-faced sergeants in charge of us were worse than any frustrated school teachers had ever been. At least there had been a let up from them when the four o'clock bell went: in the WRAAF they were always with us, picking on our slightest mistakes and finding our softest spots to prod and hurt.

I had always loved being a redhead until I joined up, but I came to hate every reference to my hair colour, which seemed to make me stand out like the one black sheep in the flock. It didn't help that I giggled behind the backs of the 'slave drivers' who, like teachers, had eyes in the backs of their heads. Anyway my hair made me popular with the men and there was plenty of them – more than I had ever seen in one place before – and I could have done with a big stick to beat them off, if I had wanted too.

The horrible sergeants; the boring drilling and ugly uniform caps were the downside but they could not come close to outweighing the upside. The camp was only ten minutes' bus run away (or lorry if we scrounged a lift, which we nearly always did) from Blackpool and we spent all our passes there.

It was paradise. Every time I smell chips and vinegar I am back, walking along that great prom – as many as ten of us linking arms and singing or shouting after the men who followed us like bees after honeysuckle. The dance halls were like something out of one of those Hollywood films about rich planters in the Deep South, all carved pillars and ceilings so high you could hardly see them, with fat-bummed cherubs flying around the edges. Vicky would have called it vulgar, but I thought it was the best place on earth. I lapped it up, couldn't get enough of it, became addicted to it.

Blackpool!

When we were handed our first home leave passes, Sergeant Parsnip, (her name was actually Parsons, but I had given her the nickname and it had stuck) actually stretched her lips into something that looked like a smile, until she came to me.

"I hope you'll apply yourself to your work more seriously when you get back Wallace," she snipped. "The Women's Royal Air Force is not a marriage bureau, it is a career!" I managed not to grab her by her scrawny throat and strangle her, but I enjoyed a quick flash of it in my mind.

Before I could even rattle the knocker on our door, Vicky threw it open. She had about a thousand curlers in her hair and her face was as white as the whitest thing you can imagine, snow, milk, whatever.

"Oh, thank God you're here!" she said. "I thought I was going to have to get Mammy to be my best maid. You said you would be here on Thursday. What happened? Oh, never mind – as long as you are here." She rushed off into the middle room and I closed the front door and went to find the rest of the family, crowded into the kitchenette as usual.

Wee Jay was sitting on the floor, eating a lump of coal (he had discovered the treasure trove of the bunker), Billy was crawling along, being an ambulance. Maggie was sitting on her usual perch on the boiler. Roddy was helping Conn to count out a mountain of three penny bits, sixpences and shillings, which he had just spilled out of a wooden box with a slit in the top. Mammy was over the sink, peeling potatoes.

"What's going on?" I asked. I was thinking of going into a huff about no one saying they were pleased to see me but I could never stay mad enough to stay in a huff, so I didn't bother.

"Your sister and that big clown are getting married at the registry office at five o'clock, that's what's going on. Your daddy'll kill her when he gets back. You're the best maid and our Conn is the best man. It's bloody ridiculous. People'll be thinking they have to get married."

"I am not going to be best maid in this grotty uniform (I had loved it a few weeks ago) and my hair's as straight as a poker. She should have warned me. "I'm not doing it," I said, ready to have a good rant about not being asked etc, when the door to the middle room opened and Vicky stood there.

I had always known she had a touch of class about her, although I would never have admitted it, but there she stood, in that dingy lobby, beside the shabby coats hanging on the rack, and she lit up the place, like a slim blue candle flame.

Maggie was the first to speak. "You're beautiful, like a film star," she said and I could hear the tears in her voice. Vicky gave a kind of embarrassed pose, holding her skirt out and curtsying. Her cheeks were pink and the blue of her suit, like a summer sky, made her eyes seem blue, although they were usually dark grey. She did look like a film star yet I was not jealous of her looks that day. She was like a little girl all dressed up for her first grown up party, but I couldn't see Big Terry being anywhere near the perfect partner.

"I'm going to look a bit stupid next to you in the photos in this stupid old uniform," I said, laughing so that she would know it didn't really bother me.

"There's not going to be any photos," she said, Terry says they are too dear. He says there's better ways to spend our money."

That was the anthem for the rest of the wedding. Everything Conn and I suggested – like going for a drink, to a hotel afterwards – was answered with the same words, "We've better ways to spend our money." Sometimes Terry said it; sometimes she did.

All the neighbours, except the Watsons, lined the close to give them a send-off. For once Terry looked presentable in a grey suit Vicky had bought him. He had a really good build, with broad shoulders and a slim waist – it was the only good thing about him, and for once he did not act the clown, but just handed first Vicky, then me into the hired car and told Conn to sit beside me, while he sat with his arms around Vicky's shoulders. The crowd shouted the usual good wishes: "Hard up," and "Good luck!" and Terry actually threw a handful (not a very big handful) of copper coins to the kids who had gathered for the 'scramble'.

Maybe it will be all right, I thought as I looked at the way she burrowed into him and saw him squeeze her arm – so hard she gave a squeak – maybe he wasn't so bad.

When we came out of the registry office, I looked for the car, thinking maybe it was parked further up the street, but it had only been hired for the one trip. It didn't bother Vicky – well didn't seem to – that Terry led us all onto a tram car, heading for the town centre.

"We're going to see that new Rita Hayworth picture," she said, "and then we'll get a fish tea. Frank and I are staying at his auntie Florrie's for the night. We'll give you your fare back to Govan."

"How about one drink before we go to the pictures?" Conn asked, "I'll go halfers."

"There'll be no drink," Terry grunted. "I've never touched the stuff, and anyway you're too young to drink. We've better ways to spend our money."

The picture was one of those awful American ones with the silly little woman standing up to the big strong man, who eventually carries her off swooning into the bedroom. I couldn't help thinking of how strong my big sister used to be before she met Big Terry and how she seemed to have turned to half-set jelly since then.

The fish tea, in a grotty little café, goes down in my memory as 'my most embarrassing moment'. The food was great. The fish and chips tasted as only Glaswegian Italians can make them and it was real butter on the bread, but Terry's antics took all the good taste away. He talked to the fat, ugly waitress as if she was some sort of precious lady, helping her with the plates and calling her 'hen', as if he had known her all his life and practically ignoring us, apart from grabbing Vicky's little bony knee in a grip which made his knuckles and her cheeks go white.

"Did you know your sister is wavery kneed?" he asked us every time he did this and she said,

"Stop it Terry, everybody is looking at us." I saw him squeeze her hand so tight several times that I felt sure that blood would start oozing out from her fingernails, yet she did not draw her hand away. This must be what people mean by 'Scotch love', I thought. It was an expression the girls in the work had used when a couple had been cruel or hurtful to one another, meaning they did it to hide their true feelings. If this was it, I certainly didn't want anything to do with it. My hand wanted to lift a fork and pin his red, hairy hand to the oilcloth table cloth before he could hurt her any more, but I knew whose side she would take in a fallout between Terry and me.

One final action made me realise that it would take all my willpower to keep the fish tea in my stomach. When we had come into the café, Terry had been chewing at something. I saw him put his hand up to his mouth and remove whatever it was. I thought it must be chewing gum, but it wasn't. As Conn and I watched from under our lowered brows (I had nudged him to watch), he removed a fingernail from his mouth and (I know this sound unbelievable (, hung it over the top of his ear. That was bad enough but what was worse was, that at the end of the meal, he removed it and put it back in his mouth.

It became a continuing fascination for the family to watch this performance at every meal he ate in our house. None of us ever mentioned it to either him or Vicky, but we speculated about it among ourselves.

I think it's something to do with witchcraft," Billy suggested. Him and Maggie were totally obsessed with witches, ghosts and things since they had learned about the Murrays upstairs having spiritualist meetings.

"He just does it so we'll ask about it," was Maggie's solution, and "He's just a nutcase," Roddy and Conn said together. I had no idea of the reason for the strange habit; it just amazed me that anyone as fussy and ladylike as my sister could tholl it in the man she was going to live with. She who left the room if anyone farted audibly!

The wedding feast over, Conn and I left to get the subway home and the newly-weds went off to spend their first night with Auntie Florrie – a toothless little woman whose body all seemed to have fallen to her bottom end and who was the only one of Terry's relatives who accepted Vicky into the family.

Conn and I plucked up courage to walk brazenly into a pub on the way. He didn't have a clue what to ask for, so I did the ordering, from a barmaid who had the yellowest hair and the most wrinkles I have ever seen. I ordered a gin and it for me (all the girls at the camp drank those) and a pint of heavy for Conn. His eyes were like stalks when the barmaid put it down in front of him. He whispered to me, "It'll take me all night to drink that."

"It had better not," I answered, sipping at my gin, in the role of Lauren Bacall. "I'm going to have another before we get the subway. Drink up. This is meant to be a celebration." Poor Conn! I've never seen anyone bring up so much as he did when we got off the subway at Govan Cross. By the time we got to number 16 he felt fine and we were singing like two linties.

At least we gave Vicky a good send off into married life. Mammy just laughed and told the two of us to get to our beds.

I lay and sang to Maggie, who was sleeping at the same end of the bed as me now that Vicky was gone. She guessed my impersonations of Guy Mitchell and Jo Stafford, as always, and giggled hysterically at my description of the fish tea and Conn's performance outside the subway station. She did have a funny smell, like musty bread, but I missed her more than any of the family when I was away and I lay and worried about what her life would be like when my leave was over. I knew that I would maybe never share a bed with her again because I had met somebody that I hoped would take me away from the Wine Alley for good.

I didn't want to be one of those girls who went into the forces only to find a man, but I couldn't help it if I just happened, a week before I came on leave, to meet the man who had made me want never to lose sight of him.

So maybe Vicky would not be the only one leaving the Wine Alley for good.

Vicky and Nancy – the new look

CHAPTER FIVE

I'm Walking Behind you

Nancy's Wedding

"Nancy wants you to be bridesmaid, but I don't know where we're going to get the money to buy you a dress. Vicky says she'll pay for her own, she's to be matron of honour."

Mammy had been worrying about 'where we're going to get the money' ever since Nancy and Buck (short for Buchanan) had said they wanted to get married as he was expecting to get posted to Korea pretty soon. All I could think of was me in some elegant, long dress, maybe velvet, with shoes and maybe some kind of wee cape to match. My imagination painted me as a cross between my idea of Tess of the D'Urbervilles and Debbie Reynolds, with everyone gasping when I walked into the church.

It didn't happen anything like that, of course.

Daddy brought home two lengths of 'silk', one peach and one a lovely soft green. Vicky nabbed the green and I was taken, with the peach, to a wee woman in a shop at the top of Govan Road, who did dressmaking. She took out a big pattern book for us to choose from but I couldn't concentrate for watching the flakes of powdery skin which kept falling from her hands on to the page as she pointed out what she thought would be suitable for a young bridesmaid. Then I had to strip to my pants and vest while she measured me.

"My, we are becoming quite the young woman," she simpered as she held her inch tape across my breasts, like spider's ankles, depositing some of her skin on my vest as she did so. I wondered if she would eventually flake away like the flour on a morning roll. She held the material next to my face to show me how much the colour would suit me. What I say in the mirror was a stick of Edinburgh rock, with scarecrow hair, not the bridesmaid I had imagined myself to be.

A week later I had to go back to be fitted and she kept sticking pins into me instead of the material and giving a squeaky little laugh.

"Sorry pet, oops, sorry pet." Still the dress felt lovely to touch and it didn't look too bad, with a large Peter Pan collar, fitted bodice and long, quite full skirt. It made me look 'quite the young lady', as 'powdery hands' said.

The next ordeal to be got through was a thing called a Marcel Wave, which was a kind of perm, which must have originated in some medieval torture chamber, but for the sake of causing gasps of admiration in the church, I would have gone through anything.

It was done in a crowded back room of the men's barber shop and the first thing you noticed was the overpowering stink – rotten eggs, babies' nappies and ammonia blended into a bouquet to strip the lining of your nostrils and make your eyes water. Your hair was rolled tightly, so tightly that you felt the roots being pulled out of your scalp, into some kind of hot poker-like contraptions and left to sizzle until it was the right degree of frizziness to please the hairdresser. Mine took ages, and every time she unrolled one of the contraptions she tut-tutted.

It was worth every agonising, burning minute of it. I looked like a film star, I thought, even with my crooked teeth, which were shown in a new smile I was perfecting, copied from a model I had seen on the front of Vicky's 'Woman's Weekly'. Looking back at the wedding photos it looks more like a grimace of agony, but I flashed it a hundred times that day, thinking it made me look really bubbly and grown up.

Nobody in the family looked like themselves on the day of the wedding. Daddy had bought himself a new, dark grey, suit which made him look more like James Cagney than ever, with his slicked back hair and a tough-looking, but nice, face. Mammy had a brown sun-ray pleated skirt and a cream blouse with a soft, floppy bow at the neck. For the first time in my life I realised where we all got our good looks from, she was so fragile and beautiful, with her black hair, straight apart from the little cheek curls that she wore when she was 'dressed' and her grey eyes shining with pride.

Conn and Roddy had on matching brown chalk-striped suits (their first) and looked so young and handsome that I felt like crying. Billy had grey flannel shorts, a new white shirt and a fair isle pullover. He seemed to have forgotten how to stop grinning, although I knew that his shyness was killing him and he wished it were all over. Wee Jay had on the neatest pair of corduroy trousers, a yellow shirt and a fair isle pullover like Billy's. He had a grown up haircut for the first time, his red, golden curls thrown into the barber's bucket as if they were nothing.

I came out of the middle room, adjusting the little, flowery pillbox which Vicky had made for her and I to wear, matching our dresses, mine peach, her's green, on top of my Shirley Temple curls. I expected gasps of admiration for my swanlike transformation but all I got was:

"You can see our Maggie's brown knickers through her dress!" This came from Vicky who stood there like a peppermint dream goddess in the flowing green skirt she had made, topped with a very simple, pure white, high-necked blouse, and it made the boys point and laugh at me.

Feeling the confidence crushed out of me like water from a jumper put through the wringer, I rushed back into the room and threw myself on the bed, face down, as I had seen Bette Davis do in one of her pictures, being careful not to wrinkle my dress.

I heard someone rummaging in the sideboard drawer.

"Come on, put these on, mind they're only on loan." It was Vicky holding up a pair of white, silk briefs which she had taken out of the drawer (I thought she had taken all her stuff away with her when she left, but there were obviously some treasures still there. I pigeon-holed a plan to have a good look later – after all it was my room now).

"Come and see Nancy before they leave for the church. You and Terry and Mammy are in the second taxi. Hurry up and get changed." I waited until she had left the room and changed my knickers. We Wallaces never undressed in front of one another.

I spoke in a sigh that nobody heard. "You look lovely." As I saw Nancy standing in the middle of the living room, surrounded by the whole family yet seeming to be on her own I tried to think of a film star she reminded me of, but there was no one beautiful enough. Vicky was footering at the back of the dress, pulling at the waist and smoothing the train (I wondered if she was thinking of her own wedding).

I knew I would never again look at a bride without comparing her unfavourably to my big sister who was perfect on that day.

There was no brazenness or smugness about her. She looked vulnerable. Shy and uncertain, as if she was relying on someone to tell her what to do next. The cheeky, forward Nancy had gone away for that day. I suddenly knew why people cry at weddings – it's not for the sadness, it's for too much beauty.

The dress was hired, a long sleeved, modest, ivory silk, young girl's dream of a dress, with a long train trimmed with delicate lace, which I was told to hold up as we went downstairs, and arrange it in the bridal car. I felt a wee bit sick at all the things that could go wrong from the house to the road outside the close.

The veil, which was borrowed from an aunt, must have been woven by spiders. It was so fine it reminded me of the webs that cling on the leaves on the hedgerows on damp summer mornings. I hoped it was not so easily destroyed with a touch.

Nancy's face was that pure whiteness that only redheads ever have. I noticed just one or two freckles on her nose and knew she would be mad at them for showing through, and her hair was the shade that the word Titian was invented for.

It was the first wedding I had ever been to, far less having an important role to play and I was so keen that I almost walked into the vestry of the church in front of the bride and groom. Somebody, probably Vicky, grabbed me and hauled me back to my rightful place in the procession. They were being married in the vestry rather than the main church because none of them had 'papers'. I wondered if I had them but I couldn't think who to ask.

The minister was youngish, with thick, dark hair and teeth like a horse. He wore glasses with tortoiseshell rims, which made a little red ridge on either side of his long, sad nose. He performed the ceremony in an absent minded fashion, due to the fact he could not take his eyes off Vicky and kept smiling at her when he should have been looking at the bride and groom. I nudged her and dislodged a giggle which she had obviously been trying to keep a prisoner and saw his face going red as he nearly dropped his bible. He fumbled and stumbled through the rest of the ceremony and I remember hoping that he hadn't made any mistakes because he had fallen for the matron of honour.

As we waited at the vestry door for the taxis that were taking us to the photographer's studio, he came over to where Vicky and Big Terry were standing and – there's no other way to describe it – started to chat her up.

"I haven't seen you at the church…" he began, looking like the wolf in Red Riding Hood when he says 'all the better to eat you with' my dear'.

"It's a bit far from where we live," she simpered at him, but Terry was having none of it.

"Ma wife and I don't go tae church," he grunted. "We've other things to do with our time." The minister laughed and shook his head as if he was a child who had said a naughty word.

"Now, now," he said, I'm sure you could both get a lot out of being involved with the church, it's not all just hymn singing and sermons you know. There's something for everybody," and still not giving up as the taxis drew up and Terry took Vicky's arm. "Do come along. You'll be so welcome." Vicky looked really pleased. Terry scowled all the way to the studio.

It was just a bare room, one wall papered, the others with flaking distemper and plaster. The hems of our dresses were grey with dust after just a few seconds. The photographer was a 'wee bloke' Daddy had met in the pub. He fancied himself as a photographer and we were his first wedding group. (Probably his last too I should think). He was a dwarfish, porridge looking excuse for a man, with wispy ginger hair, eyes that looked quizzically at each other and a musty, kind of hospital smell about him.

"Right the young couple first," he said in a voice that seemed to come from a few feet above his head, herding Nancy and Buck to stand in front of a panel draped in an old curtain. He caught

Mammy looking at the curtain and assured her. "Don't worry hen, it comes out really good as a background."

It didn't take him long to get all the different groupings and it was arranged that he would come to the reception at number sixteen to take a photo of the wedding party plus their guests who had not come to the ceremony.

On the way home we all sat in silence, scared to attract Daddy's attention. It was obvious by his high colour and eyebrows hooding his eyes like an angry owl, that he was not in a very good mood. I kind of pitied the photographer if the photos turned out as bad as we all thought they would, but this was not the time to mention how I felt.

Everything brightened up when we saw the spread laid out in our living room. Mrs Freckle had excelled herself. She had baked the wedding cake, tarts, shortbread, butterfly cakes and other goodies. On top of this Mammy had ordered a whole board of small cakes and teabread from the Co-op (it was in the big bedroom to be kept for replenishing the dishes as they emptied). There were pyramids of little triangular sandwiches, bridge rolls and hot sausage rolls that we smelt as we were coming in the close. Everything was laid out on a long table (hired from the Co-op) covered with the whitest tablecloth ever. Mrs Freckle stood just inside the kitchen door holding an enormous brown teapot, the same colour as her hair.

"Everything's just ready to serve," she said. "I'll leave you to it and see you in the morning." This was a hint that she would be looking for her money for the purvey in the morning, but I didn't know that at the time.

I was meant to help with the serving up, giving people plates and paper napkins and handing round sandwiches to the guests, but I soon abandoned this when I saw Billy eating his fourth sausage roll and decided I should look after myself and let the guests do the same.

I was sent into the room with two cake plates and told to fill them up from the board. When I put the light on there were two figures sitting cross-legged on the floor, stuffing their faces with cake. Roddy had brought wee Jay in as his accomplice and they had eaten about a dozen between them. I sat with them for a while and joined in before taking through a selection of what was left. A whole board of cakes, just sitting there alone in a bedroom, was bound to be attacked in a house full of hungry children. Nobody ever knew.

Everything was cleared away, the tables folded up and put out on the landing. The wedding cake put in the kitchen to be cut up later and put into lovely little paper bags Nancy had bought to give to the friends who had not been able to come to the wedding. (She told me that she was going to tell everyone that the cake she was cutting in the wedding photos was 'only the bottom tier' but it was the only tier), and the chairs, such as they were, arranged around the walls – we were ready for music.

Some late guests arrived, some of Daddy's younger cousins and an aunt or two. I was constantly running to have a pee with excitement and I had to keep checking my legs in their first pair of nylons (held up by knicker elastic) in the wardrobe mirror in the big room. I had changed into my kilted skirt and white blouse, the long dress was too uncomfortable for enjoyment. I thought that I looked really good, although the wrinkles at the backs of my knees annoyed me a bit. My legs were just not curvy enough for nylons and I would have liked to have a more grown up blouse instead of the plain shirt-like thing I had. I contented myself by shoving two hankies into my liberty bodice and opening the top two buttons of the blouse before opening the living room door and just standing there – Bette Davis always did that – and waited for the offer of a dance.

His name was Jimmy Osborne and he was the best looking man in the room. He was wearing an immaculate grey suit and a Persil-white shirt that dazzled my eyes. He had red hair – all Daddy's relatives did – but much darker, more auburn than Nancy's or the rest of the family's and tanned skin as opposed to the ruddy look of the other redheaded men I knew and he had really long eyelashes – like the picture of a camel I had seen, and dark brown eyes. And he was pulling me close to him for a dance!

It was one of those mad Scottish dances, where the main purpose seems to be for the men to manhandle the women and swing them about until they lose their footing. It was like being on the Waltzer, only better, because I had never been so close to anyone before, far less a man. Two fears were spoiling it, that the hankies would pop out of the top of my blouse, and I would pee myself, but I didn't get to worry for too long. Suddenly I was being pulled from my partner's arms and I saw a fist I recognised, missing his chin and hitting him on the shoulder. He put an arm up and caught the next blow.

"What the hell's wrong John?" he asked Daddy who was staring at him like a bull at a gate it's about to demolish.

"What have I done man?"

"You're mauling a wee lassie of thirteen. That's what you've done. You're mauling my daughter." He made to have another go at him but the other men held him back.

"John, for God's sake!" I heard Mammy shouting from somewhere around the fireplace.

"Come on into the room." It was Nancy, white-faced but kind of laughing as she took me away from the scene. I was a bit annoyed. There I was, the centre of a scene that happened all the time in the films and I was not to take any more part in it.

After about ten minutes we heard voices in the lobby and I peered out of the bedroom door to see Jimmy and the girl he had brought with him, being shown out of the door by Mammy, who was shaking her head and tutting as he shook her hand.

"It'll be all right," she said. "See him when the two of you have sobered up."

We went back to the party and no more was said about it. I wondered if I would ever see Jimmy again. I had a great dream about him that night.

It was not a dream when I next saw him, more like a most embarrassing moment of nightmare proportions.

I heard a deep voice as I came in the front door from school, followed by Mammy and another woman laughing. One thing I loved was visitors, so I threw my books in the middle of the room, had a quick look at myself in the mirror and strolled into the living room. He was there, sitting at the table with Mammy, Daddy and a plump, glowing girl who smiled at me and touched Jimmy's arm as I stood there. I guessed she must be the girl he had brought to the wedding but I paid no attention to her so I was not sure.

He turned in his chair and looked at me, at my shiny-bummed gymslip, at my shabby school blouse and squinty tie and my obvious schoolgirlishness and the blood began to rise under his skin, from the collar of his blue shirt to the roots of his dark auburn hair. He turned from me to Daddy. "This isn't…?" he asked. "God I'm so sorry John and you May. It must have been the drink. She's only a wean." He shook his head and looked down at the table.

The girl squeezed his hand and said, "Wheesht Jimmy, it's all forgotten."

Nobody spoke to me so I just turned and went out the way I had come in. I sat for a long time, leaning out of the bedroom window and just letting the tears run down my face. I could still hear them laughing and talking in the living room.

It wasn't just the humiliation and my enjoyment of dramatics that was making me cry. I was missing Nancy already. She was off to married quarters in England, where she would stay for a few weeks until she left the WRAF. Then she was moving to London to stay with her in-laws, as Buck was being posted to Korea. I felt sure I was never going to see her again and wrote in my School Friend diary:

"Had a great time at Nancy's wedding. Daddy punched a man for dancing with me. I'll never forgive her husband for taking my sister away from us to live in England. I miss her already."

*

So that was that, one more of the Wallace family had left the Wine Alley. I thought Conn would be the next because he was expecting his National Service papers as soon as his apprenticeship was up. Things would never be the same again.

Roddy and Cann

CHAPTER SIX

Conn

We were only there half an hour when I was in my first fight.

There were a few lads kicking a ball about the street when we came out of the close mouth and we stood and watched them until one of them passed the ball to me. I passed it back and followed it out onto the street. I sensed there was a ritual to be performed and hoped I was doing the right thing.

"Want to play five-a-side?" the smallest of the group asked. "Is this your wee bree?"

I nodded to both questions and they gathered in around us, their eyes pecking curiously at the new jackets Daddy had bought us, and travelling down to our shiny, black school boots, like baby birds of prey, sizing up their dinner. I took my jacket off and placed it down as one of the goalposts and Robert did the same at the other side.

"Right, Shug and me'll pick our teams," shouted the wee lad. "I'll take you big yin. What's your name?" None of them wanted to pick Roddy, but eventually he ended up on the same side as me, our captain was Alec Cuthill, he lived in the same close as us.

It was good. I felt I was going to like living here. They were a great group o' lads, except for the swearing, which seemed to be every second word and there was one lad who seemed to hate Roddy on sight (probably the red hair) and kept picking on him. I just waited for Roddy to lose his rag.

It happened when the lad, who was a lot older and bigger, kicked the ball right at Roddy's stomach. When he got his wind back he leaped onto the other fella's back like the old man of the sea in the Sinbad story in one of Maggie's books. Unlike Sinbad he had no trouble shaking him off and Roddy landed sprawling on his back at the bully's feet.

That's when he did the awful thing. The thing that made me want to kill him.

"Right wee cheuchter," he shouted. "You think your gonnae get away wi' jumpin' on me do you?" He leaned over and I thought he was going to hit him – I was ready to pull him off if he did, but I knew Roddy didn't like me fighting his battles. Two of the other lads were holding my arms, but my anger gave me the strength to shake them off, when he suddenly turned and sat down on my brother's face.

The noise of the fart against his face turned me into a maniac. It was the most shaming thing I had ever seen and it had been done to my own brother. The rest of the lads were pointing and laughing as he sat there screwing his face up like a baby filling his nappy and let rip with another. Roddy kicked and struggled but he could not get from under that disgusting arse.

I walked over quite slowly and grabbed the bastard by the ears. He screamed as I lifted him by them and then threw him to the ground and landed myself on top of him. I could see nothing. All I knew was that my fist was going like a piston at his head and the hands he was trying to use to protect himself. I didn't give him the chance to hit back. I wanted to kill him, to rub out my brother's shame.

Daddy came into the street at just the right time for both of us. He pulled me off the lad (we found out later his name was Korky) and lifted Roddy to his feet. He was retching and boaking all the way up the stairs, but he wasn't crying and I knew he would be planning his revenge – as was I.

"Go and get yerselves cleaned up," Daddy said when we got in the house. "This is going to be nipped in the bud right now. I'll not have a pair of street fighters living under my roof. I've seen enough fighting to last me a lifetime, and I'll not stand for any more of it."

We went into the bathroom together and washed our faces and hands. Poor Roddy kept blowing his nose into big chunks of toilet paper as if the smell was still in there and he had to get it out.

"You'll blow your brains into your hankie if you keep that up." I laughed when I said it, hoping to make him laugh too, but he looked as if the misery and shame had permanently scarred his face.

"I want to kill that big pape," he said, scrubbing at his mouth and nose with the towel. "He should have let us finish him off, so he should."

"Come in here you two!" Daddy shouted from the kitchen.

We expected a cuff on the ear, although I never remember him hitting any of us, or a big long lecture, but he didn't even look angry as he spread margarine on two big outsiders of toast and put them beside the cups of tea he had poured.

"Bring your stuff through to the living room," he said, "and we'll sort this out."

He wanted to know why I had been trying to kill the other guy, so I told him what he had done to Robby, although I felt sorry for making him ashamed all over again.

"Bastard!" he said. "I should have left you to it." He stood up and took his jacket from the back of the chair and put it on.

"Right, come on. We'll fix this right now." He turned and looked at me just as we went out the door. "Can you beat this fella in a fair fight?" he asked. I nodded and he turned to Roddy. "You just stand back and listen. Keep your head, d'you hear me?"

The lads were all sitting about the low wall that bordered the front 'garden'. Some of them jumped up when they saw us coming out of the close mouth – ready for fighting or running, whichever was called for.

"You don't have to run away lads. I just want to talk tae the lad that picks on fellas weeer than himself – who is that then?" Their eyes answered his question as they turned in Korky's direction.

"Oh, it's you is it? Come here a minute son," he said, taking Roddy by the shoulder and walking him over to stand beside Korky. He stood back and looked from one to the other as if comparing their sizes, and then laughed and shook his head; he kept looking from one to the other like this until everybody was laughing. Korky looked ready to greet or burst.

"Wee sissy," he blurted out. "Getting his da to fight his battles for him. He shouldnae play wi' the big lads if he cannae take it." Daddy walked over to him and grabbed him by the scruff of the neck, at the same time pulling me forward.

"He's only half your size, ye big drink o' water," he said quietly. "But his big brother here is willing to take you on in a fair fight. What do you say to that big man, eh?"

My guts were rumbling like thunder and my hands were sweating but I felt like doing a boxer's dance around my opponent. I felt good.

"Well?" Daddy gave Korky a shake as if he was a pup who'd just wet the floor. "What's it to be? Apologise for that disgusting thing you did to the wee fella or get your lights beat out by somebody your own size. Make up your mind – our tea's about ready."

"I don't want to fight." It came out as a croak – no wonder, he was nearly being strangled. "It was a joke. I'm sorry."

"Let everybody hear you then." Another little shake.

"I don't want to fight. I'm sorry." He struggled out of Daddy's hold and ran away up the street, into a close about five away from ours. Not one of his pals went with him, instead one of them – I think it was Shug, kicked the ball to my feet and shouted.

"Come on – three an' in. You're in goal first Tommy!" and everybody took up their positions and waited for me to pass the ball. I looked round for Daddy and he was watching from the close mouth wearing the same mad grin that our Billy often wore.

I knew we would be fine in the Wine Alley after that.

I was used to fighting Roddy's battles. I didn't care about that. It's what you do in a family. You stick up for one another, even if you don't get on that well, you don't let anybody else say anything bad about your family or beat them in a fight. Mind you, it could be hard going with Roddy, because he was the worst nark you ever met.

"Our Roddy would cause a fight in an empty house," Mammy used to say, and she was right. He was much smarter than any of the crowd we hung about with, although most of them were my age or older, and he had a way of making them look stupid with a smart remark, or picking an argument about nothing (He disputed every goal that anybody ever scored except himself) that made people want to batter him and if they were bigger I had to stop them.

Yet he and I never fought each other. I think it was because we had such different natures, but we had slept in the same bed since we were wee weans and never seriously fell out. I think he was a wee bit scared to push me the way he did to the other lads, but he never did.

I was glad I could fight and everybody knew I could, although I didn't look for fights, but it made up for all the sissy things I had to do, like look after my wee brothers and sisters and, worst of all, go for the messages on a Saturday morning, standing in the queue at the grocers with a lot of wee fat women, who sometimes took my place in the queue; while Roddy stood in the queue at the butcher's and glared at anybody who dared to speak to him.

There were perks. We always got a 'wee skin' off Mammy's change – not too much, that would have been lousy to do that – cheat your own mother – just enough to get fags and a pie at halftime when we went to see the Rangers on a Saturday. That was one of the great things about the Wine Alley, it was just about ten minutes' walk from Ibrox Park, and we could go to every home game.

Daddy took us the first couple of times, but after he went away we went ourselves. It was quite cheap because there was a special 'boys gate' and usually we could get somebody to lift Roddy over the turnstile, so he didn't have to pay. The first time I saw this (it was Daddy that lifted him) I spent the whole match waiting for the polis to arrest us, but I soon found out that it was accepted and nobody minded weans being lifted in for free.

That first week in number 16 was crowded with 'firsts' for all of us: the first inside lavatory and real bath; the first fight (for Roddy and I); the first sight of the fattest woman in the world; the first visit to Ibrox Park; the first living up a close; the first day at new schools (for everyone but Nancy and Vicky). That was one I was hoping to avoid. When the others wondered what their schools would be like, I kept quiet, hoping that I would be forgotten and left out of the plans. It wasn't that I hated school more or less than any other lad of fourteen, I just hated the thought of starting a new one when I was just a few months off leaving for good.

On the Sunday night, Mammy had a big fire lit, right up the lum, to heat the back boiler so that we could all have baths and be clean for our new schools in the morning. Roddy and I had new grey trousers and shirts and were to wear them with our 'lumber jack' jackets that Daddy had bought us, which were an invitation for people to pick fights with us, and Daddy stayed in and gave us army haircuts.

We were all prepared for another first.

"Now, what about this fellow?" Mr Williams, the headmaster, looked over his half-glasses at me, trying to look friendly, but really looking like someone who has found half a worm in an apple he's just bitten. "What are we going to do with him?"

"He was in his last year at the big school in Ballantrae," Mammy said. "I've to take him to the High School this morning when I'm finished here and see if they can take him in."

"Hmm, the High School." He studied me for ages and then said, "What were you good at in your last school young man? Anything?"

The wound in my stomach clenched like a fist. I hated this man.

"English was my best subject, but I was ok at arithmetic and history and geography and I was the best footballer in the school." I told him.

"Hmm, what about practical subjects, woodwork, metalwork and so on?" he asked ignoring what I had said. "A boy like you, you'll be looking for an apprenticeship when you leave…" he gave a little laugh. "English, history and geography won't do you any good there and you can play football in your own time, unless you're another Willie Waddell." He sneered kindly.

Mammy looked at me and plucked up courage to say to him, "His dad wants him to go to the High School. All of his family went there and if they don't have a place for him, we'll try Bellahouston…"

He didn't even let her finish, but began shaking his head, "Lassie, lassie," he said, reducing Mammy to a silly wee girl who had suggested something really stupid. "Bellahouston is out of the question. We have trouble getting our brightest ac-a-dem-ic pupils in there and even if he did get in – which he won't, he would feel really out of place." I wanted to grind his stupid glasses into his face; my stomach was throbbing and the acid was flooding into my chest making it burn like hot pepper. I stood up and Mammy did the same – I think she thought she might have to stop me from hitting him.

"There is a very good solution to the lad's problem," he said, sitting forward in his chair. We stood there looking at him, waiting for more insults: "We have a very good Advanced Division at this school, which would suit a boy like your son perfectly. It concentrates on teaching *practical* skills, preparing boys for *work* rather than further education. Take my advice m'dear. You couldn't do any better for him."

I was out the door before he had finished, but I heard Mammy saying, "Thank you for your time, I'll see what his father says."

*

"Advanced Division?" he said, looking at Mammy and I as if we'd broken out in bealing scabs. "What is that supposed to be? Did you take him to the High School?"

"I told the headmaster I would see what you thought," Mammy said. "I suppose I did the wrong thing as usual. Someday I'll do something right."

"Oh don't start that," Daddy said. He had just come in from work and as usual she handed him his tea and the paper as soon as he sat down. It was a ritual that nothing ever interfered with. Then she told him how she had got on with getting us into school. She started with the wee ones and Roddy.

Maggie and Billy were in a composite class, which would be good for them as they were used to being together and Roddy was in the 'qualifying class', although he was a bit younger that the rest, but he would probably be smarter. She told him it was an old building but it seemed to be a really good school and the teachers seemed to be very nice. Then she told him about me and the Advanced Division.

"I don't need anybody to tell me what it is," he said. "It should really be called the Backward Division. It's for dumbos who have failed their 'qually'. Most of them probably cannae read or write. They wouldnae even get an apprenticeship – they'll be the midden men and road sweepers. I'll keep him off school before I'll let him go into that, it's as bad as the Special School. Take him to Govan High tomorrow, or I'll take the day off and take him myself."

So, I got into Govan High, into 3T 1. That meant the emphasis in my education would be on technical subjects. They too decided that an apprenticeship would be my ambition for the future. I guessed it must be. Still, there were more interesting things coming into my life than school.

At last we could do more than just listen to Rangers on the wireless, we could see them at least every fortnight. Another thing, there were a lot of good looking lassies in Kellas Street – a couple in our own close, opposite number 16. When we heard their name was Broon we rolled about on the bed laughing, but Lizzie and Jeanie looked nothing like the 'Broons' family in the Sunday Post. They were smashers, especially Lizzie. I'd never really been interested in lassies before – all that stuff seemed a bit sissy to me – but Lizzie changed all that.

Another good thing about us all living together in the Wine Alley house was that we had our big sisters back. I'd missed them when they went away to live with Granny Ross, especially Nancy. Vicky and I had never got on, in fact we had some really bad fights at times. She said I was a clipe and I said she was a snob, but I had still missed her and was glad to have her back, even though she was always sniffing at Roddy and I when we took our shoes off and picking on our appearance and the state of our room, clothes, hair and even the way we talked. I had still missed her.

Nancy was different, she had always been more of a pal to us, like another brother in a way, joining in our apple and tomato stealing when we were evacuated – even hiding the tomatoes up her knicker leg when we nearly got caught one time. We were all kind of in awe of Vicky I suppose, being the eldest, and she did keep herself kind of apart from us, sending out waves of disapproval at us.

Roddy, Nancy and I even made up imaginary names for one another, which nobody else knew about. She was Tilly (pronounced Tiddy), I was Poty and Roddy was Tinna. We secretly called the rest of the family Mudda (Mammy), Dill (Vick); Boy Will (Billy, Dill Mags (Maggie. We didn't have a name for wee Jay as he wasn't a person yet. It was a daft game maybe, but we kept it up all the time we were growing up and even after. We still went out with Nancy quite a lot. She took us to the pictures sometimes and it used to make me blush when fellows stared at her and whistled and chirruped, but I felt quite chuffed just the same. It was another one up we had on all the other lads in the street – having two smashing looking sisters.

Like everybody else, I couldn't believe it when Vicky, definitely the best looking lassie in the street, took up with Big Terry next door, but I was too busy leaving school, looking for a job and falling for Lizzie Broon, to worry too much about it.

*

The Broons didn't have a mother. There was just the dad, Harry, and his two daughters. He'd brought them up since his wife had died when they were just weans, something that made him a bit of a saint in the eyes of the close women.

"No every man wad bring up two wee lassies oan his ain," I often heard one or another of them saying, as though it would have been expected of him to have abandoned them. Their attitude puzzled me for a long time until I got used to the differences between men and women in Wine Alley.

Men were gods, who could get away with almost anything and women were put on Earth to look after them and do what their men told them.

Harry Broon was different in a lot of ways. He treated his daughters as his equals. No – more than this – as his superiors, and did what they told him, as long as it was something he wanted to do anyway. He didn't seem to have a job, as he always seemed to be in when I used excuses to go to their door in the hope of getting a chance to talk to Lizzie, without being observed by my pals, or even worse, the close women. He went from close to close selling 'things' – pictures of sailing ships or dancing girls made from silver paper; comic books, toffee apples and homemade tablet, which the women bought out of their kindness to him.

Every Friday and Saturday night, he toddled into the street, drunk and usually happy, singing to himself and waving up to all the windows, even those not occupied by a 'hinger oot'. He was the first man I had ever seen with a 'Ronald Coleman' moustache and I decided I would have one as soon as my reluctant beard began to show through my, so far, barren skin. I wanted to know him nearly as much as I wanted to winch his daughter.

Lizzie and Jean were as different from the young people in the street as their father was from the people his age. They only spoke to the other lassies and lads if they spoke first and, like their dad, they didn't have jobs, although they had left school.

I found out that Jean was fifteen and Lizzie was seventeen, two years older than me, but that didn't put me off. I pictured our first date: me putting my arm around her waist as I took her into the pictures and all the corner boys drooling with jealousy as we passed. Her looking up into my eyes, the way Lauren Bacall looked at Humphrey Bogart. I was having so many wet dreams about her I was even considering how I could wash our sheet without Mammy knowing, and Roddy was beginning to make remarks about my 'nightmares' in a kind of snide voice, which he used when he knew more than he was admitting.

"The Broons are having a party on Saturday night, are you going?" Shug asked me when we were sitting in the back close sharing a tiny wee dout he'd nicked out of his dad's pocket.

"I suppose so," I answered. "Unless I'm going elsewhere." I couldn't tell him I hadn't been asked, but he put my mind at ease on that:

"A crowd o' us are gonnae gatecrash," he said. "It'll be a scream, so it will."

It turned out I didn't have to join the gate crashers. Lizzie and Jean were leaning out of their window the next night when I came back from the café with Daddy's fags. "Hi you!" Jean shouted. "Come here a minute. We want to speak to you. What age are you?"

"Sixteen." I could feel the heat rising in my face and lisped, as I always did when I was nervous.

The two girls nudging one another and giggling didn't help. "You can come to our party on Saturday if you like," Lizzie said and slammed down the window.

For once I didn't tell Roddy what was going on. I knew he would sneer and probably come with me.

I sneaked away before the match was finished on the Saturday – I told him I was going for a pish – and went home and got ready and left before he got back.

"I spent half an hour looking for you. Wherever have you been?" he moaned when I finally crept home. I had to tell him what had happened then. It was bursting out of me and I didn't care that it would give him something to torment me with forever. It had to be told, if only to get it clear in my own mind.

I had put on the new trousers and white shirt Mammy had got me for my job interviews and one of the silk ties that Daddy had given us, with a dragon embroidered down the front of it. I tapped ten bob off Nancy and got a box of chocolates and a packet of fags to take with me. She was quite excited when I told her I had a date (I didn't tell her about the party – she thought the Broons were hairies) and she combed my hair into a DA at the back and knotted my tie in a Windsor knot – she said that was all the go at the dancing.

I hung around in Alec Cuthill's bedroom, letting on I was interested in his model airplane collection, but all the time watching, first for Roddy coming back from the match and then for people arriving for the party – I didn't want to be the first and look like a silly wee boy, even though that was how I felt.

About seven o'clock, Roddy came back out of the close. He stood playing keepie-uppie for about ten minutes and then went off with the Curries, up to the park.

For a fraction of a cowardly second, I wanted to go after him and avoid the dangers of the Broon girls, but as I watched the other fellas and lassies going into number 10, two by two, I said cheerio to Alec and hurried across the road, hairy bits already itchy with sweat.

I didn't know anyone in the Broon's living room, which had been arranged much the same as I'd seen ours done when Nancy and Vicky had had their parties: the chairs and a couch pushed back to the wall, leaving a space in the centre for dancing and the usual games – winky, subways, postman's knock, spin the bottle. There was one big difference about this party – there was drink being handed round along with the cakes and sandwiches.

"Don't tell your ma." Lizzie said as she handed me a half pint tumbler filled with what looked like Irn Bru, smelled like Irn Bru and tasted like sickly sweet fire-water.

It was fire-water. One of the fellas worked in a whiskey bond in Partick and had brought a couple of bottles of the 'real stuff' – unbonded whiskey. All you needed was an eyedropper full, topped up with 'girders' to get as drunk as honey bees on nectar.

I was glad I forced myself to stop grooing at the smell long enough to get it down – although my stomach wanted to throw it right back up – because it gave me the courage to sing when the bottle stopped spinning at me, and that made me the hit of the party, because if there's one thing I'm good at, it's singing.

I sung a Frank Sinatra song 'Nancy with the laughing face' and everybody clapped and cheered, especially the lassies. Lizzie jumped on me and kissed me on the lips. "Ye wee smasher!" she said. "A didnae know you could sing an a'." I sung another couple of songs and then one of the fellas (they were fed up with me getting all the attention) suggested a game of Postman's Knock. When the numbers were being whispered around, Lizzie whispered to me.

"Come into the kitchen for a minute."

Hand in hand we bypassed the kitchen door. I had a quick flash of a lassie sitting up on the edge of the kitchen sink with her white legs wrapped around a fella who was making noises like a pig.

"In here wee son," Lizzie whispered, shoving me before her into an untidy bedroom, which smelled damp. Jean was sitting on the bed.

They sat on either side of me and Lizzie handed me another drink, which went down much easier than the first. My tie was loosened first and then my shirt was off (I was glad I hadn't put on a vest) and all the time they were undressing me their hands were fluttering over me and they were taking turns kissing me. I could hear the party carrying on far away, like a distant storm, but the storm in my mind and body gradually blocked out even the distant sound, as I sunk into the lumpy bed and gave myself up to the two sisters.

I did struggle a bit when I felt my trousers being removed over my ankles, but Lizzie was using her tongue in a way that made me unable to move. All the time I could hear this weird moaning, as if someone else was in the room with us. It wasn't until Jean said, "Sssh, no sae loud son," that I realised it was coming from me.

It wasn't the first time I had cum, far from it. Apart from my 'nightmares' that Roddy had found so funny, I had done it for my pals and they done it for me and just lately we had found a 'daft' girl in the school who would do it for anybody and even give you a look inside her knickers, as long as you didn't tell – of course everybody knew about her.

This was swimming with dolphins compared to paddling with tadpoles. These two sisters had the most amazing hands and mouths; when they made it happen it seemed to go on forever, my body jerking like an epileptic and the stuff spurting from me like a pot of milk boiling over. They were laughing as they watched me, but I wouldn't have cared if they had whistled Dixie, I had left all shame and respect behind and I wanted it to last forever.

When it was over I curled up and went to sleep and it was well into the night when I woke up and crept back across the street to number 16. Lucky for me Mammy had left the key in the door for Nancy, so I could sneak in without anyone knowing – except Roddy, who was lying awake in the darkness.

"Did you get your hole?" he whispered from the depths of the blankets. I told him I'd tell him all about it in the morning and got into bed, turning my back to him and pulling the blankets over my head. I didn't feel so good any more.

"There's a funny smell off you," he said. "You stink."

I lay staring at the light from the street lamp outside our window for a while, and then nudged him awake and told him everything that had happened. He groaned and tittered throughout, till I thought he was going to cum just at the telling, but when I finished and turned back away from him, he put a question that gave me something to think about for a long time.

"Did they no' let you put it in?" he asked. "I mean that's no really getting your hole, is it?"

I had no answer. I often return to that question, even now I wonder what the Broon sisters got out of it that night.

*

The Broon sisters didn't bother with me after that night, they didn't even send me for their fags. Lizzie got married to a right brute a few months later and he moved in across the road and Jean went to stay with her granny in Partick and just visited sometimes at the weekend. The close women said Lizzie's man beat her up and sometimes did the same to Harry. Whether it was true or not, Harry seemed to creep about; he'd lost his style and become another old drunk, while Lizzie, as beautiful and desirable as ever in my eyes, was often seen sitting at the entrance to the close crying her eyes out when the brute – a corner boy called Billy Palmer – had thrown her out.

I had dreams of going over there and taking her away to safety, like John Wayne would have done, but there was no John Wayne to help poor Lizzie and a sixteen-year-old boy can't mourn one girl forever. I had other interests.

After Daddy had left for Singapore, I knew I was the man of the house. It made me feel quite old, knowing that, but I was determined to get a job as soon as I left school – to prove that I was a man; bringing money into the house every week, like other men.

Roddy and I were still close, but him being still at school, kind of cramped his style when it came to the dancing or the hunt for lumbers – anyway his teachers were writing to Mammy that he should be allowed to stay on at school and do highers and go to university. He was getting more big-headed by the day and getting into more fights because of it.

"Is that really what you want to do?" he asked when I got word that a local engineering company were taking me on as an apprentice. It wasn't. I wanted to be a famous singer or actor, but I couldn't tell him that after his reaction when I told him I was joining a youth club that put on plays and had talent shows once a month.

Daddy wrote that he was delighted that I had joined the youth club. He always wanted us to join things. He thought it would keep us from being 'corner boys' as he had been before the war. The three things he told Roddy and I we should always remember – before he left Mammy to bring up the lot of us – were: get a good apprenticeship, don't hang around street corners and respect lassies. The first two I had achieved by my sixteenth birthday. As for the third, I was too scared of them to treat lassies with anything less than respect.

*

Life in the Wine Alley was pretty good. The job was not as bad as I had thought it would be. I had been picked for a part in the play the club was putting on and I had met a wee smasher at the dancing that I was plucking up courage to ask out.

Vicky's announcement that I have to be best man at her wedding was like a kick in the stomach and I had to rush to the sink and throw up my tea.

It had been my favourite too – stew and doughballs.

"You'll be the laughing stock of Govan," Mammy spat at her in her anger. "Getting your wee brother to be best man. He's just a wee boy. Has that big clown got no pals that could do it? They'll all be Catholics I suppose."

Vicky's face was chalk white, but she had that stubborn look that we all knew. I felt sorry for her, although we had never really liked one another very much, and the thought of doing anything as manly and grown up as being best man, put me on her side.

"Am not a wee boy," I said. "I'm working and bringing in a wage. If Vicky wants me to be best man, I'll do it." Mammy drew me a disgusted look and slammed out of the room.

"Who's to be bridesmaid?" I asked, already picturing a romance for myself.

"I'll ask our Nancy," Vicky said. "She's coming home on leave the day before."

I'll never forget the wedding.

It was next in the horror scale to the time when I was in hospital (the cause of my gut trouble) and I had to ask for a bed pan while the ward was full of visitors. It wasn't so much the asking for it – it was the sight of everyone trying not to inhale the smell after they removed the screens which were meant to preserve my dignity.

My first feeling on the day of the wedding was pride as I looked at my two beautiful sisters – Vicky in a dress the colour of the sky, looking so fragile and beautiful and Nancy in her Air Force blue uniform with her red hair and fantastic figure, looking like a film star. I looked darkly handsome, as they say in 'True Romances' which was Roddy and I's favourite reading at the time.

Poor Big Terry! My second feeling was pity for him, having to be compared to three such good looking people as us. Vicky had tried her best to turn him into a handsome groom. He had a great build and the suit she had bought him showed it off; his hair, which was wiry and thick had been neatly cut; his shirt was gleaming white and his shoes were polished, but his eyes seemed to be more red and piggy than usual. I knew he couldn't help the sore eyes, but I couldn't forgive him for not being the handsome groom Vicky deserved.

I wanted to hit him when he squeezed her arm so tight, she gave a little yelp like a pup being stood on, and when he was all over the fat waitress in the café, but, once the happy pair went off to spend their wedding night in Terry's aunties' house, Nancy and I had a great time. She bought me a couple of pints that made me sick but it was still a great time. We all really missed her being away in the WRAAF and it was great to have her home on leave.

*

I don't know when I first knew I could sing. I remember singing 'When I grow too old to dream' to my great granny before I started school, so it must have been very early in my life. I just took it for granted. I was always first to sing at parties and when the crowd of us fellas and lassies got up a sing-song as we sat at the close mouth, it was always me that everybody shouted for. I don't think I was big-headed about it. I just knew that I could sing. And of course I remembered the effect my singing had had on Lizzie Broon!

"Haw Conn," Sadie Ranachan shouted to me between songs. "You should go in for that competition in the Plaza. I bet you would win."

Roddy kept on at me to go in for it. The prize was ten pounds for the winner and a place in the next heat; five pounds for the second and two pounds for the third. I had never even seen ten pounds and pictured myself swaggering into the living room and pouring gold coins into Mammy's lap or taking the whole family to the seaside. I had no idea what ten pounds would buy, but I knew I wanted to find out.

The drawback was my stomach.

As soon as I thought that I had got the nerve to go to the box office in the Plaza and get an entry form, some devil started knitting my guts together and I knew I would spew right there in the foyer in front of the posters for next week's main feature. Finally, Roddy went and got the form, filled it in and handed it to the girl in her little glass cage.

*

The talent show was put on before the big picture. It wasn't just singers, you got would-be comedians, jugglers, Al Jolson and Charlie Chaplin impersonators and, the night of my heat, a classical dancer.

One of the two Al Jolsons opened the bill with 'Mammy', he was rubbish but everybody loved Al Jolson since they had seen the film of his life story and they cheered his impersonator like mad. Next was a juggler who kept dropping his Indian clubs, finally having to go off after one of them had drawn blood from his head. Then another Al Jolson, singing 'Sonny Boy', making all the old women in the audience greet.

There was a Chaplin, a comedian and a magician before the classical dancer floated in from the wings on the tips of her toes. While I was laughing with the rest of the audience, I kept thinking 'poor lassie, she thinks she is good'. Maybe she was good and we were just a crowd of ignorant pigs. She certainly got the biggest laugh of the night. She was dressed in a kind of flowing thing, like a net curtain, that showed her knickers and she had the biggest muscles on her calves that I had ever seen. She leapt and twirled, waving her arms as if she was throwing something on the stage and kept a po-faced expression from start to finish, which was a splitz, with her hands held up to the heavens as if she were waiting for the applause – instead she got sweetie papers, ice cream cartons and jeers. As she looked up from her wonderful bow, I saw tears running into her mouth and the look of hurt surprise on her face that she had danced her heart out for people who much preferred Al Jolson impersonators.

It was my turn next. The last turn of the heat. My stomach was knitting a jumper. The MC had been on and picked up the rubbish and quietened down the animals who now had a taste for blood.

"Don't know why, there's no sun up in the sky," I began.

Someone shouted, "Sing up son," and was wheeshed by other voices. I took a deep breath and gave it laldy.

'Stormy Weather' was a hard song to sing but I knew I was good at it. The knitting needles in my insides stopped clicking and I just sang.

Everybody said I should have won, but I didn't, one of the Al Jolsons did and Roddy nearly got into a fight with his brother when we were leaving the hall. I was second and had a fiver in my pocket and a taste for performing. I would win the next time. That was the start of my way out of the Wine Alley and I knew I was going to take it.

I didn't want Daddy to know. I thought he would laugh and call me a Jessie. It was Maggie that told him.

"There's nothing wrong wi' trying to get on," he said. "As long as you remember your trade comes first. Singers are ten-a-penny but a good engineer will never be out of work."

This was part of the beliefs he tried to give us as we were growing up. We were not like the other weans in the Wine Alley, we had a future, we had to stick in and learn a trade, education was the key to everything (The house was full of educational books he had bought us). We did not hate Roman Catholics but we should remember that their religion is evil.

I got into bother with him a few times because of my bosses complaining to him about me. I was always late in the mornings. I just hated getting up and even worse, the foreman found out I was going to the afternoon session at the Albert Ballroom, when I was meant to be attending day release at Engineering College. I nearly got sacked that time. Daddy managed to persuade them to give me a second chance.

"He's a good worker," the foreman told him. "But he has no ambition. The firm pays for our apprentices to go to college and we don't want to waste money on somebody who's not interested."

I was a couple of months off my eighteenth birthday, so I felt like a big shot when he told me he was taking me for a pint. I'd had the lectures, from the foreman, the tradesmen, the college principal and now I guessed I was going to get the daddy of them all from him, but I still felt pretty proud at being taken out for a pint with my old man. We'd all felt much better since he came back from Malaya.

It was Friday night and the pub was mobbed. It was like the Red Sea parting the way the crowd at the bar moved to let him through and the barman shouted to him right away, "Half and a pint, Johnnie? What about the boy?"

"The same for ma son," he answered and I felt as if my chest would burst through my shirt buttons.

"Come up here, where it's a bit quieter," he said when we had our drinks, leading me to a space at the end of the bar. "Slange," he said drinking his whisky in one long gulp.

"Slange," I answered and tried to do the same. When I had stopped coughing, he told me to drink some of my beer, slowly. "Whisky takes a wee bit practice," he laughed.

"Your sister tells me there's another singing competition coming up," he said, lighting a cigarette for himself. He didn't offer me one. What's your chances?"

"I think I've got a good chance at winning the Glasgow heat. The final's in London.

"Right, I'll tell you what I'll do. I'll get you a' the new gear, suit, shirt, tie, the lot, for the competition, but you must promise to stick in at your work. No more sneaking off to the jiggin' and learn to be on time. Nobody likes bad timekeepers. I bet Sinatra disnae lie in when he should be at work. What do you say to that?"

What could I say? If there had been room in the bar I would have done a cartwheel, as it was I stuttered, "It sounds great. I'll not let you down."

"Right finish that up and away you go out wi' your pals – you're cramping my style."

He gave me a wink and blew a perfect smoke ring, which to my imagination seemed to float above his head like a halo.

*

The talent show was to be held in a big, old picture house in the Gorbals. It was called the 'Palace' and it looked the part, if you imagined a palace to be like the inside of an egg, painted in red and gold, with obese cherubs aiming arrows at one another from one side of the domed ceiling to the other. The curtains and the seats were dark green plush and it had the same wonderful smell as the subway, overlaid with a hint of sweat and ice cream. I was dazed by that smell, as a wee man in a green, shiny suit with gold fringes on the shoulders and peaked cap with gold braid, resting on the back of his head, showed me and the other contestants around, in the afternoon of the night of the show.

"This is the biggest picture house in Glasgow," he said. "And we're no tied tae any of the big distributors so we can show what pictures we like. There'll be no big picture the three nights of the talent show – just cartoons and the news – so youse better be good."

He took us into a wee, dingy office at the back of the projection room and the MC – a has-been Glasgow comic – told us the order we would be appearing; asked us a bit about ourselves for his 'patter' when he introduced us and introduced us to the pianist, a tortoise of a man who reeked of Eldorado, who took over from him and discussed our music. When I told him I was going to sing a Frank Sinatra number, he flashed his brown teeth with delight and gave me much better treatment than he gave the rest of the contestants.

"Frankie's the wee boy," he said. "He's a great chanter."

The show was to run over three nights, Thursday, Friday and Saturday and the winner from each night was to go down to London, all expenses paid and compete in the semi-final and, if we got through, in the final, it was on the Friday.

I hoped my stomach would not let me down. I was going through enough Rennies to cure an elephant's indigestion.

Daddy came in early on the night of the show. He was half scooped and there were tears in his eyes as he made me stand there in the living room in my new, dark blue suit and white shirt (He had wanted to get me a bowtie but I had persuaded him a silk knotted one was better) and sing my song just for the family – I didn't want any of them to come and watch me perform.

I sang 'My Nancy with the laughing face' and he shushed Mammy for joining in as the tears dripped off the end of his nose and as soon as I was finished he walked out of the room without a word, just grabbing my hand and ruffling my hair as he passed.

Like a big Jessie, I felt like crying as well; was I that bad?

Mammy explained. We always knew he had been brought up by his granny because his mother had died. We didn't know until that night, that he had also had two wee sisters who had died, called Maggie, aged five and Nancy, aged fifteen.

I don't know if knowing about the girl who would have been my auntie Nancy made me feel the song more deeply. I only know I sung it better than I had ever done before and the audience, particularly the women, went mad for me.

I won.

I hadn't let any of the family come to see me winning but they all left me to the train for London, except Nancy, who was going to meet up with me there and Vicky wouldn't come without Big Terry, who was working (he said).

My Wine Alley days were coming to an end, I hoped.

CHAPTER SEVEN

Anything Goes

RODDY'S STORY

The train couldn't go quickly enough for me. Glasgow! I knew we belonged there instead of that wee stupid, country yokel, village we'd lived in while Daddy was away. The only thing that hadn't been boring about that place was stealing apples; setting fire to the gorse bushes in the park in the middle of the village; taking the yokel's money off them at cards and guddling salmon in the river, that was owned by some big English toff in London. I used to say to Conn, when we were in bed at night, that when I was rich (I never said if), I would buy the village and the river and have all the yokels who had ever called us 'Glesca Keelies', working for me for next to nothing.

I could see that Conn's guts were bothering him. He had been sleekitly sticking Rennies in his mouth since we got on the train, but I knew he was looking forward to the big city as much as me. His memories of living there before were clearer than mine, I had only been four when we left, he'd been six.

As usual him and I had to carry nearly everything when we got off the train. The subway terrified me. It was great and people were friendly to us, as if they had known us before and were glad to see us back.

That's what Glasgow people are like all the time – except when they think you are being fly or looking down your nose at them, or they don't like your religion. I really felt that this was where we belonged and I was dying to make new pals, go to a real school and best of all, go to see Rangers at Ibrox every week.

Hope we won't be living next to too many papes, I thought, but it didn't worry me too much. Conn and I could handle them. There would be fights at first until they got used to us, but we would soon make pals. All the locals in the village had looked up to us, I know that.

The new pals didn't happen right away, in fact a war nearly broke out.

It was fine at first. After we got our tea, we went out into the street and a crowd of blokes asked us if we wanted to join in a game of 'three and in'. I waited to see what Conn would do. He took off his new, plaid lumberjacket and put it down for a goalpost, so I did the same. (We hated these jackets that Daddy had bought us. They made us look like right country yokels – better to look like a leper than a country yokel).

The game went on fine for a while, both of us scoring our three goals and then taking our turn in goal, until a big, lanky fella started picking on me. I was shouting for him to pass the ball, when he stood back and kicked it with all his strength – right into my belly. Through the sound of me trying to get my breath back, I could hear the rest laughing and shouting, "Fucking wee tcheuchter! What's up wi' ye? You told me to pass the ba' tae ye?"

My first thought was to kill him.

I took a running jump onto his back but I tripped on the siver and he got me down on my back. He was too heavy for me to get from under him and he was sitting right on my face when he let loose a big, dirty fart. The taste and the smell of the gas from his insides was like dead cats and rotting vegetables. The more I tried to push that fat, papish arse off me, the louder they all laughed and, encouraged, he let go another that made me boak, as if my stomach wanted to turn inside out. Just when I thought I was suffocating, he was pulled off me – Conn had lifted him by the ears and was now sitting on his chest, getting laid into him.

I knew Conn had a temper but I had never seen him like this. The big pig tried to cover his face, but he wasn't caring where he hit him as long as he did. There were sparks of blood flying from his nose. I wanted to join in but I couldn't get past Conn's mad fists.

Lanky's pals were circling around, kidding themselves that they were trying to help him by pulling Conn off, but they were all too scared to get close enough. A murder might have been done if Daddy hadn't got back from the pub. He pulled Conn off and told the two of us to get up the stair.

We were sure we would be kept in for fighting, but he just told us to go and get cleaned up. When we came into the kitchen he had made tea and two big 'outsiders' of toasted cheese. My nose was red raw from the blowing I had given it, trying to get rid of the taste – it was more a taste than a smell – of that pig's gas and Conn's knuckles were grazed.

"Sit down and eat your pieces," Daddy said, "and tell me what this is all about. You're only five minutes in the place and I have to stop a fight. I've had enough of fighting in my day, so I don't want you two starting. D'you hear me?" He took out a fag and lit it. "Well I'm waiting. You wouldn't be getting laid into that fella for nothing, son come on – what happened?"

I tried to signal to Conn not to tell him in case he would laugh at me the way the lads in the street had done, but he kept his eyes away from me as he told him. Daddy didn't laugh. He stood up. His face had gone pure white.

"Right, finish your tea," he said. " We better sort this out now."

It was great the way Daddy made such a clown of Korky – that was the rotten pig's name – by making him stand beside me, to show how much bigger he was (I still thought I could beat him in a fair fight) and making him apologise or fight Conn. He apologised and then ran away like the big Jessie he was. At first I thought the other blokes would leave as well. They stood and talked to one another for a while and then a boy, called Tim Curry, kicked the ball to Conn and said, "Right, come on, we'll get on with the game. Whose turn is it in goal?"

We never had any bother after that. I was chuffed that they were all scared of Conn but I wished they didn't think I always needed him to fight my battles. One thing I was sure of, I would get my own back on Korky, if it took twenty years.

As it turned out it took only two.

Him and I had become quite pally – well he thought so – and this night I saw him staggering up the street. He'd been to a party and he was stewed.

"Come on big man," I said, taking his arm. "I'll help you up the road." He didn't even know who was talking to him and leaned on me as we turned into his close. I let him go, just at the steps and he fell and rolled over on his back. I straddled my legs over him. His eyes were trying to focus through the alcohol fog and his nose and mouth were dripping with spittle.

"Wh... what the fuck's goin' on?" he spluttered and I was tempted to kick his teeth down his throat. Instead I opened my fly, I'd been bursting for a pish for ages, and let go a Niagara Falls, waving my willy around like a garden hose, making sure every bit of him, eyes, nose, mouth and his good Sunday suit, got a good watering. The smell wasn't just as bad as the one he had inflicted on me, but it would take much longer to go away.

He never mentioned it to me but I felt much easier about being pally with him after that.

I always had this thing about getting back at anybody that annoyed me or got one over on me, no matter how long it took. It happened just before I left primary school to go to the High.

We were the only weans from Wine Alley that went to Ibrox school. Everybody else – scruffs and dafties – went to Broomloan Road, the so-called 'ragged' school, but Mammy and Daddy thought we were too good for that (They were right) and sent us to Ibrox, although the old headmaster wasn't very keen to have us. Billy, Maggie and I went there, Conn went to the high.

I was put straight into the qualifying class, although I was nearly a year younger than the rest of them. That never worried me, I knew I was smarter. Colin Mackie, a wet blubber of a lad, was 'top of the class' and Miss Lynn the teacher sat me beside him so he could 'show me the ropes'. That made me laugh for a start. If he was top boy, I thought, I must be a genius!

Everybody thought that he would win the top prize for the qualifying exam. It was a gold wristwatch that was donated by some big-wig ex-pupil. I felt a wee bit sorry for him, knowing he didn't stand a chance next to me, but I just let him go on living in dreams. He would know the bad news soon enough.

The qualifying exam – the results decided whether we went to one of the two high schools in the area, the junior secondary, or stayed on in the 'advanced' division (for total tubes) – was a walkover for me. I was sitting with my arms folded while the rest of them were still sticking out their tongues and chewing their pens.

When the results were announced, just before the summer holidays, I came top in everything, at least five marks ahead of specky Mackie. His face went scarlet and he rushed out of the room. Miss Lynn told me, with a smirk, that I could have had full marks but three had been deducted for poor handwriting. I knew this was balls but I didn't care. I had won the watch and that was what I wanted.

Nobody in our family had ever had a watch, not even Daddy himself.

All the prize winners were given a letter to take home to their folks – an invitation to see their weans being presented in front of the whole school and local big shots.

Mammy opened it and just said, "Good," and put it on the mantelpiece for Daddy to see when he got in from work. It was a Friday and, as usual, he was a bit later than on other nights and loaded down with sweeties and fish suppers for us. Once he was sat down on his chair with his tea, I reached the letter down from the mantelpiece and handed it to him, expecting to be praised to the skies.

"What's this?" he asked, shaking the letter at me. "This is no good enough!" I thought he was joking and began to laugh. "Do you think it's funny?" he growled, putting his plate down on the floor and sitting forward in his seat.

"What?" I asked, still with a silly grin plastered on my face, like a mistake you can't rub out.

"All these weeks you've been telling us you came top in everything in your qually; that you were getting a gold watch, and all the time you're only second. I hate lies. Did you think we'd never know? Where was the watch tae come from? Were you gonnae steal it, or what?" He threw the letter at my feet and I bent to pick it up.

There it was, in Miss Lynn's copperplate writing – the list of prize winners:

FIRST PRIZE FOR ACADEMIC ACHIEVEMENT – Colin Mackie.

SECOND PRIZE FOR ACADEMIC ACHIEVEMENT – Roddie Wallace.

I couldn't read any further. I knew it was a mistake. I knew I had top marks and I knew the whole family thought I was a liar. I sat awhile with the letter crushed in my hand, not able to speak, as Daddy scraped his tea into the fire and lit up a fag. It was as if he didn't want to look at me – and then:

"I didnae tell lies. I got full marks for the qually. They only took three off me for poor handwriting because they don't believe in giving anyone full marks. I didnae tell lies," I said. "It must be because Mackie's the teacher's pet.

"Right," he said to Mammy. "Get me some writing paper and an envelope. I'm not having anybody belonging to me cheated out of a prize he deserves, now you're sure you didnae lie?"

"I didnae lie," I repeated, beginning to enjoy being the centre of attention, and in the right. That gold watch should be mine and the worst thing had been that I felt the teachers had beaten me.

They liked Mackie because he was a slimey sneak and agreed with everything they said. They hated me, particularly the Head. He never wanted us in his school. He'd said as much to Mammy, that day he gave her a red face, when she took us to be enrolled. And, on top of that, I had put him right about something at school assembly one morning, in front of the whole school.

He had been chunnering on about Bonnie Prince Charlie one morning – God knows why – about how he had been a great Scot's hero and a' that – and I put my hand up to ask a question (He likes weans to do this. It showed they were paying attention).

"Well Wallace?" he said, with a kind of smirk in his voice.

"Please sir?" I said, putting a real worried expression on my face. "I read a book that says Prince Charlie wasn't really a hero. Was he not a coward for running away when his country was in trouble?" I thought everyone would turn to look at me, but they didn't. Most of them, the weans that is, kept their eyes to the front – on Mr Williams, who looked as if he had swallowed lavvy water. The teachers started walking up and down the rows as if they expected us to riot. It reminded me of a prison picture I had seen, with Burt Lancaster.

"Trying to be smart as usual Wallace," he eventually said and I'm sure the first two rows got a bath with his spittle. "To most Scottish people, Prince Charles was and still is a great National Hero (He said it with capital letters). What some third rate book says will not change that. Maybe you think some footballer, like William Waddel or George Young, is more of a hero?" Now all eyes were on me, waiting for my answer but he didn't give me a chance. "Some of us believe there are things more important than football. My office after assembly Wallace."

He nodded to where Tarzan, the music teacher, was sitting paralysed at the piano and his twiggy little hands crashed down on the opening bars of the march that always played as we scuffled to our classrooms.

In his office, he wouldn't even let me speak, just havered on for ten minutes in a cataract of words, about respect: respect for your elders and betters; national pride; not being too big for your boots and the certainty that I was heading for a 'bad end'.

My punishment was to copy out, ten times, two pages from a history book, that made Prince Charlie look better than Jesus Christ, instead of the weak coward that I think he was. I didn't do it and he never asked me for it.

I was thinking about that as Daddy sat puffing away and busily writing on the writing paper he had sent Maggie down to the shops for. He covered three pages, sealed it in an envelope and wrote Mr Williams name on it. "You'll take this to the school on Monday, and tell him you've to wait for an answer," he said and stood it up on the mantelpiece, from where I felt its presence all weekend.

For once I was dying to get to school on Monday morning.

I told the secretary that I had a letter from 'my father' for the headmaster. She held out her hand for it and I said I was to give it to him personally. She tutted several times and took me through to his room.

"Wallace to see you Headmaster," she said as if what she really meant was. "A piece of rubbish to see you Headmaster."

But with that letter in my hand she was dross under my feet.

As he read the letter his face went from red to white, to puce and back again.

"Go to your class Wallace," he told me. "I will write to your father."

"Please sir," I said, screwing my feet to the floor. "He said I've to wait for an answer."

"You'll get the answer when I have time to write it!" He stood up and pointed to the door. "Go to your class and I'll send for you to collect it before four o'clock.

As I went out the door, I heard him saying to the secretary, "This is what happens when you let people like that send their children to a good school."

He sent for me just before the bell went at four o'clock and handed me a letter in an Education Authority envelope, without saying a word.

I knew Daddy had a temper, I had seen him throwing his own brother downstairs for swearing in front of us weans, but when he read that letter, it was spectacular! He even swore himself.

"Jesus Christ," he said. "The bastards! Is this what we get for being stuck in that hole away frae ma family for a' they years?" throwing the letter into Mammy's lap. " I'm goin' up to that school in the morning. I'm gonnae clear the place. I'll frighten the shit out of the snobbish bastards. I'll make him choke on his bloody watch."

Mammy was shaking her head as she read the letter – I wished she would let me see what was in it – and I could see her hand shaking as she held it.

"Do you think you should do that?" she asked. "After all he is getting a prize, isn't he. And the other boy has been longer at the school than him…"

He cut her off before she could say any more. "That's typical of you, trying to please everybody, never wanting to stand up for your rights. No wonder they're growing up like sissies. I'm telling you, I'll be at that clown's door first thing in the morning. Have I got a clean shirt?"

He was there. He walked up to the school with us, people staring as we went into the playground, hoping for something exciting to happen – and marched right up to the Head's door.

He was off sick, if you could believe that. He'd left the deputy head – a wee quiet lady, who always wore the same green, tweed costume and walked about on her tiptoes all the time – to explain the situation to Daddy.

She told him that the gold watch wasn't a prize for just the qualifying exam, but for the whole year's achievement and as I hadn't been there for a whole year – although I had been top in the exam – I was not entitled to the watch, but I was being given two really nice books and a certificate.

The thing was, Williams had counted on the fact that no one could be rude to Miss Napier and where Daddy was concerned, he was right.

"I didn't want to upset her," he said. "She's seventy if she's a day and what she said made sense in a way." He aimed a pretend punch at my nose. "Never mind son, there'll be other prizes. I'll get you a gold watch myself as soon as I've got a few bob."

I couldn't take it. I never could take losing. It wasn't the watch, anymore, that tormented me, it was how to make Mackie suffer for winning it.

The primary seven teacher always took her class on an outing in the last week of term – it was a kind of tradition. That year it was to Ayr. We were to visit Burns' cottage at Alloway and then spend the rest of the day on the beach. I made sure I sat next to Mackie on the bus, terrifying him with my friendliness at first, but before long I could see he thought of me as his best pal and that was just what I wanted.

He was wearing the watch. "Ma says I've to keep it for good," he said as I admired it for the millionth time. "But she let me wear it for today seeing as it's a special occasion."

"Let me try it on, just for a minute," I begged, disgusting myself. At first he shook his head, so I turned away from him and began speaking to the lads across the passage, depriving him of his new friend. I knew exactly how that would make him feel. If I hadn't sat beside him, nobody else would. Nobody wanted him for a mate. I was well-liked and they all thought that I should have got the watch. It was a shame for him really, but it's more important to look after number one than feel sorry for people.

He nudged me in the back I had turned to him. "OK, you can try it," he said. "But just for a minute, eh?"

It was when I stood up to wave the streamers out of the window that the terrible accident happened. Somehow the catch on the window got caught in the watch strap and pulled it from my wrist onto the flashing road.

"Oh my God, your watch!" I shouted, waving my empty wrist at him. "It got caught in the window. I'll get the driver to stop the bus." He did stop, but by the time Mackie and I ran back along the road all we found was a trail of bits of watch: a strap, some springs, an unbroken glass and a sad, twisted, wee face, which looked awful like poor auld Mackie's. He was greetin' like a wean and I felt a mixture of pity and satisfaction. He hadn't deserved the watch anyway, so I made sure he didn't get it.

I helped him pick up the pieces and wrap them in his hankie, saying a hundred times how sorry I was. I nearly felt bad when he said, "It was an accident."

There wasn't a lot of kids from the Wine Alley went to the High school, but I was one of them. Just as I started my first term, Conn had left and was starting his engineering apprenticeship. I really envied him. His wages weren't much and he had to give most of it towards his keep, but he was left with some pocket money. He paid me into the pictures once a week and bought the pies and Bovril when we went to see the 'Gers' but he was beginning to be right keen on going to the dancing and he was always watching the Broon lassies across the road. I watched them as well and made up my mind to have one of them as my first girlfriend, but I was only twelve and they didn't even see me.

They did more than see Conn.

I had been mad at him for sneaking off to their party without me, although I knew they wouldn't want kids there, so I kept awake until he came in. I wanted to pick an argument with him but I changed my mind when I saw him. His face was green and he was shaking like a jakey and as he climbed under the blankets I got a strong whiff of that smell I had been noticing in our bed some mornings, usually after one of us had been dreaming – mine were always about some spotty, fat lassie I hated, or a teacher with hairs on her chin – and woken us both up with the vibration of the iron bedstead.

When he told me what they had done to him, I didn't need anything to start up my wet dreams for weeks after – I just had to picture what he had told me. I wished it had been me. It was another reason to make me hate being younger.

I hated not having any money even though Conn and his pals treated me a lot. They were all working. They were men (at fifteen) I was still a boy. If I had my own money it would be different. Daddy slipped me a few bob most Saturdays and Mammy let me keep the change when I ran to the shops for her, but I envied the blokes having their own wage packet, even if they were not actually bursting at the seams with cash after they paid their 'digs'.

My pal at school, Ally Boyd, and I started a pitch and toss school in the spare ground at the back of the playing fields. It was great for a few weeks and I built up a great wee kitty in a dried milk tin that I kept behind the gas fire, with MacRobert's bayonet. It was good to pay my way for a change, with Conn and the boys, but I still had to let them pay sometimes, so they wouldn't know what I was up to. It came to an end one day when two sneaky teachers turned up in the middle of the game.

The lookout shouted a warning 'LOB' (Look out boys) but he was too slow and we hadn't time to stow all the money and take off. They had a big fat Glesca polis with them and we were sure we were for the clink, but he just made us hand over the money to the teachers and then gave us one of those boring 'man to man' talks that polis, teachers and ministers are trained in.

The Head sent for us and told us he was more hurt than angry, especially at me, because my exam results showed that I was 'university material' and he had expected better of me. We were let off with a four page essay on 'The Dangers of Gambling' and a severe warning. He said he wouldn't tell our parents this time, provided the essays were satisfactory. It wasn't really a punishment for me because I wrote first class essays, but Ally had to stay in a week to do it.

We didn't know for sure, but the word in the boys' bogs was that one of the wee toffs from the bought houses had complained to his Mummy that he had lost all his money to some rough boys from the Wine Alley. Lucky for him we never found out his name.

My kitty lasted a couple of weeks and then I had to think of a new scheme for getting money. I got the idea from a cowboy book I was reading. It was a great story, either by Zane Grey or somebody Jepson.

The US Marshall was called in to a frontier town to sort out a band of outlaws who were taking money of the 'dirt farmers' for protection. If they didn't pay, their cattle were run off and their cabins set on fire, so, being really weak and whiney, they all paid, except for one – a beautiful golden-haired girl – who had sent for Marshall McClue, who shot them all and rode off with the girl sitting beside him on his horse.

The word for what the outlaws were doing was extortion and it seemed like a good idea to me. I didn't intend to burn anybody or even hurt them all that much, but I knew quite a few of the posh lot always had money to spend. I just wanted my share of it. The baddie in the film had a great saying 'Always look after number one'. It became my saying from then on.

There was a group of third year boys, about four or five, who all kept themselves apart from the other lads in their year. They came from the private houses across from Elder Park and always wore full school uniform and carried their books in cases instead of the stretchy rubber bands the rest of us used.

One of them Eric Davy, brought his violin case to school on Fridays, when he was one of the few pupils who got music tuition. If for nothing else, we hated him for that. Him and his pals were our first victims in the extortion racket I ran, after I saw that film, until I left school.

They didn't go to the dinner school. They carried pansy wee lunch boxes and all got together in a corner of the playground if the weather was fine, or in the hall if it was raining, to eat their dinky, wee sandwiches, apples and Mummy's home baking. If it hadn't been for the teachers on 'lunch duty' we would probably have eaten them as well as their pieces, but they were safe while they stayed within the school area.

In the first and second year, you were not allowed to leave the school grounds at the interval, but in the third year upwards you came of age for visiting the tuck shop (it was just a newsagents that kept a stock of sweets and crisps for the school kids). We noticed that our prey always walked up to the tuckie after they had finished their lunch, to buy something nice for the afternoon interval – not for them the sneaky sweetie eaten under cover of the desk lid, that would have been naughty – another reason we hated them.

"I saw that jessie, Davy, changing a pound note at the tuckie this morning," Ally told me, almost slavering at the thought.

"That's the third time this week and his rotten, wee pals were all loaded too."

"Right," I decided. "We'll wait in the Gypsy's lane for him tomorrow. I bet he'll cough up if we just look like we're gonnae hit him."

"He'll likely pish his draws," Ally sneered.

The next day was Friday and our first attempt at being hoodlums couldn't have worked better.

Eric and his three chums were strolling along, keeping a good distance from the other weans making for the tuckie. He was carrying the stupid violin case – his music lesson was first period after lunch when the rest of us were getting Bible Studies – Ally rushed out of our hiding place and ran into the other three, with his arms spread like a German bomber and I grabbed for the hand that held the violin case – I knew he would hold on, so I could pull him into the close to do our 'negotiations'. My plan was to threaten to punch his lights out unless he gave me his money, but I didn't have to do that. As I pulled, he tripped and left me holding the precious violin case. He was waving his white, girlie hands around trying to reach it where I held it above my head. I heard mad laughter and realised it was mine. "Right, fiddle face," I growled in my best Humphrey Bogart. "Give me your money, or I'll drop it on the ground and jump on it."

I could see he was trying not to greet and I suppose some people might have felt sorry for him, but my motto was 'Look after number one' and that's what I was doing. He handed me a pound note and I stuffed it in my hipper.

"If you clipe, it'll be the worse for you," I warned, giving him a wee clip on the head with the case before I handed it back.

It was the easiest and best fun way of getting money I had ever tried. The feeling of power was tremendous.

Sometimes we trapped one of them in the Gypsy's close as we had done that first day; other times it would be in the toilet, two of us pushing one of the toffs into the cubicle and taking his money under threat of having his head flushed down the pan; sometimes in the cloakroom at the gym, where we would promise to throw their trousers out the window if they didn't cough up.

It worked until just before our leaving date, and they stopped bringing money to school. Maybe they had told their folks what was happening or something, we never found out why, but our golden goose stopped laying and I was skint again. Nothing for it but to take a job with the 'milk', which I did until I left school. The tips were better than my extortion racket, but I hated the early rising and it wasn't nearly as satisfying.

Conn and I still went around together most of the time, although he was totally mad about the dancing, and I felt out of place there, being that much younger than the crowd that went – too young for any of the lasses that went.

They thought! If the silly bitches could have read my mind when I walked behind them on the street they would have known whether I was too young or not.

It was me that first talked Conn into going in for the singing competitions that were all the rage in the picture houses – in the interval between all the rubbish and the main feature, or sometimes before or after the programme – and it wasn't long before he was winning. I got into a fight one night when the judges picked a lousy Jolson impersonator over him, singing 'Stormy Weather' which he was magic at, but we managed to run faster than 'Jolson's' pals and jump on the bus for home.

When the NATIONAL SINGING STARS competition was announced on the screen one Saturday night, I was desperate for him to enter, but he wouldn't go to the box office to get a form.

That was the thing about Conn, once he opened his mouth to sing his nerves disappeared, but the lead up to it was hell for him. Sometimes he was still wiping the bile from his mouth as he walked onto the stage to sing his heart out. I wished it was me that could sing. Nothing would have stopped me but when I sang at parties, people either laughed or went all quiet as if somebody had just made a bad smell.

It was Maggie that finally got him to enter. She told Daddy about it and he talked him round and promised to get him a new suit if he got past the first round and let him wear his best Donegal tweed overcoat, he had just bought, to go there on the first night.

He took him to the pub and they came back singing and laughing and told the rest of us what had been decided. I was a wee bit miffed about the suit, but I knew in my heart that Daddy wouldn't get one a suit without getting the other the same, so I was happy to bide my time. All I could think about was going with Conn to the Palace, the biggest picture hall in Britain – Daddy told us.

Every night when we were lying in bed, in the dark, I had to listen to him singing. He was between 'Stormy Weather' and 'Nancy With The Laughing Face'. I liked 'Stormy Weather' best. I thought the words in 'Nancy' were too soppy, but Conn preferred 'Nancy'.

"I don't want any of the family to come with me," he told me on the Saturday morning as we were lying in bed. "I'm nervous enough as it is. It would only make me worse."

"Aye you're right," I said, picking him up wrong. "It'll be better if it's just the two of us. The rest of them might give you a showing up, you know what they are."

"No, I mean I'm going on my own," he muttered through the bedclothes. Nothing I could say or do would change his mind and Daddy backed him up.

"If that's how you feel," he said. "It's your choice. You do it the way you want to. We'll see you when you come back with first prize."

Things seemed to be happening awful quick since we had come to stay at Wine Alley. I felt as if things were beginning and ending all the time. First Daddy had gone away to Malaya. He said it was to get more money for us but Conn and I thought it was just that he found life in Civvy Street, with a wife and weans, too boring after the excitement of the war and he hated his job in the gasworks.

Then there was the excitement of Vicky marrying Big Terry next door. I just cut myself off from all the rows about that. I was as puzzled as everybody else about her marrying such a clown – and a pape as well – but why not just let her get on with it. It wouldn't affect me, so why should I care? Conn was best man. He told me all about it later after he had stopped feeling sick from the pints of beer Nancy had bought him. He said he felt like killing Big Terry for the way he treated our Vicky, but I said she must like it or she wouldn't be marrying him.

I felt that we were like that poem, 'Ten Little Nigger Boys', after we arrived at Wine Alley. First Daddy left, then Vicky and the next one was Nancy. I knew I would miss her. She was my favourite. She was everybody's favourite. When she told us she was going to join the WRAAF, we had a ball making up stories about the adventures she would have and how we would be involved in them. But when the time came for her to go, we were like two, sill, big jessies, moping around and nearly greetin'. She came back after six weeks for Vicky's wedding, to be best maid, but I knew she would never be back palling around with us now she had made the break.

Daddy did come back, and this time to stay, he told us, and it was through him and probably me that the next 'nigger' left.

It was Conn. Off to London after he won the SINGING STARS heat. I was desperate to go along with him and be his manager when he 'hit the big time' but Daddy told me not to be daft to: "Get stuck into your school work and get yourself into university. It's time we had a doctor or a lawyer in the family." I let it go for then but I had no intention of staying at school any longer than I had to. I wanted money. I wanted to be a big shot. Lawyers and doctors are ten a penny, I thought.

When I defied teachers, Daddy and even Granny Ross, to leave school, the first thing they did was get me an apprenticeship, where Conn had started. It would do until I could find a way to get to the top. In the meantime I kept them all happy by going to day release, night school and getting the top prize for first year apprentice.

I had visited Conn in London. The big time was as far above him as the star on top of the Trafalgar Square Christmas tree. He was working in an engineering shop during the day and singing in grotty, old pubs at night. He was too good for that but the Cockney fools didn't realise it. To them he was just another Jock, coming to London to make his fortune. I went back more determined than ever to rise above these people.

I knew Daddy had brains, more than anybody I knew, but his upbringing had kept him back. He was better read and more intelligent than any teacher I'd come across, yet he was working as a metal polisher in an aircraft factory, which was a better job than the other men in the Wine Alley had but it was way below what I wanted for myself.

Our whole family were smart but only Maggie had any ambition (She told everybody she was going to be a famous writer when she grew up). Nancy had had the guts to join up but I think she thought it was a way of having a good time and meeting a lot of good looking blokes. It wasn't really ambition that drove her. Conn was the best chanter I'd ever heard, apart from Sinatra, but he would never push himself forward. The trouble was he didn't believe how good he was. You need more than brains or talent to get to the top of the tree. You need to know how to use yourself and other people. I wasn't long in learning you must find a way of impressing the bosses without losing face with the men on the shop floor.

Nobody likes a crawler, so you have to do your crawling undercover.

Another thing I learned was that women took to me and were always willing to be used, one way or another.

The work's night out was always a good time to further my career plans. Jimmy Riddock, the head foreman of the engineering workshop, was always stopping at my bench to ask, "How's the college work going? There'll be no holding you when you get that degree under your belt, eh?" I had told him, just casually slipping it into the conversation that I had applied to sit for a B.Sc. through the day release college and he'd done everything but kiss me. It was a feather in his cap to have an apprentice getting a degree from the shop floor. It was as if I was his protégé and I could do no wrong after that.

"Well, Ginger," he said as he stopped at my bench the day before the night out. (I put up with the nickname, if anyone else had used it I would have given them their head to play keepie-uppy wi'). "All ready for the do tomorrow night? You'll have your eye on one of the young lasses no doubt?"

"Time enough for lasses," I said,. putting on a serious 'young man on the up' face. "When I've got letters after my name and a good job. I'll enjoy the dance though. You have to let your hair down sometime." He looked at me as if I was his favourite dinner. I'd learned just what to say to keep in his good books. If I'd been too serious and goody-goody he would have seen me as just a bore who wanted his job, but he liked the idea of young people letting their hair down. It made him feel that nobody would see anything wrong in him patting the girls' arses and pulling them into stationery cupboards, for more than a pat. I remembered when we had guddled fish when we lived in the country, tickling their bellies until they gave themselves up and I felt I was doing the same to Jimmy Riddock, only it was his ego I was tickling. There's nothing some older men like better than being treated as 'one of the boys' and played up this weakness to the limit.

"You'll be coming for a pint wi' the rest of us before the dance?" I asked.

"Well," he was actually blushing, the mug. "I don't know if the wife would like that. You know what they're like," he stuttered, like a virgin being asked for her first kiss.

"Bring her along," I said, being damn sure he wouldn't.

"I'll tell you what," he said, glancing around to see if anyone else was earwigging. "Why don't you meet us in the bar of the hotel. My daughter's coming along and I'm sure she would rather see a young, handsome fellow like yourself than two old fogeys like her ma and me. How about that?"

I quickly went into my 'I'm not worthy' routine and agreed to meet up with them in the bar. I'd heard that his daughter wasn't bad looking. Being nice to her could do me nothing but good in her old man's book.

It nearly ruined everything. She wasn't a bad looker, but you could smell the desperation for a man coming off her – not just any man; one she could turn into a husband as soon as she let him handle her wares. It was terrifying. That must be how a fox feels when it sees the hounds coming after it. If I made one slip she would devour me. If I tried too obviously to escape (like pretending I'd taken ill or something) I would lose my 'friendship' with the boss.

From the very minute I was introduced to her mother and her, they took me over.

"Jimmy's always talking about you and how well you've done," Flora, the mother, said, putting a wee, chubby hand, deformed with rings, on my shoulder and squeezing my muscles (spiders ankles Conn called them) as if she was testing the ripeness of melons. When 'our Sadie' wound herself round my other arm, like a clinging vine, I knew a trap was about to shut its jaws on me if I didn't use my famous brains.

I asked her for the first dance. She wasn't a bad dancer but I always turned against lasses that showed they were too keen. I wanted to be horrible to them, and I usually was, but it wouldn't be a good idea to be horrible to 'our Sadie'. I saw her back to her ma and da's table and went up to the bar for another round. While I was there I asked as many blokes as I could to 'give the boss's lass a dance.

"She doesn't know a lot of people," I said, "and it can't be much fun sitting with her ma and da all night." I was pleased with the 'nice bloke' image I was projecting, although I knew I wasn't fooling anybody. Everybody knew I had my eye on the big blonde from the wages office and I got her that night, when I saw her home and her folks were in bed. It was too easy. I wouldn't be asking her out.

Sadie got me up for the ladies' choice. Her eyes were glittering and her cheeks were pink and sweaty with excitement. She was sure she was the belle of the ball. "I haven't sat down all night," she said. "My feet are lowping. I'm sorry we didn't get another dance sooner. Daddy says you can come back with us for a wee night-cap if you like?" She tilted her head in a 'Daddy's little girl' kind of way that made me want to smack her one.

"Och, that's a shame," I said. "I promised my ma I wouldnae be late. She hates being on her own when Da's on nightshift. I hope you'll ask me some other time." I rushed her back to the table and said I had to phone home, before she could think of an 'other' time.

On the Monday morning I couldn't get away from Jimmy. He kept making excuses to come to my bench, as if he was already my father-in-law and the rest of the blokes were getting really crude with their kidding.

"Here comes you father-in-law again."

"Ye must have slipped his lass one, did ye?"

"I hope she's no' up the duff," were the polite remarks and a couple of them kept singing bits of a song about 'Marrying the boss's daughter', that he must have heard but it seemed to please rather than annoy him. I was expecting it all day but I still felt sick when it came.

"The missus and me were wondering if you would like to come to the club on Friday night with us and our Sadie? It's usually a great wee night – and the drink's cheap," he blurted out as he was having a pish in the next urinal to me, after the lunch break.

"Aye, sure," I answered. I was terrified of giving his Sadie too much encouragement but I wanted to keep in with him for a wee while longer. Normally if a lassie threw herself at me like that I would go with her for a few weeks, shag her stupid – always using a frenchie – and then let her down as gently as I could. But you couldn't do that with the boss's daughter, not yet anyway.

It became a regular thing, going out with them to the club on a Friday night, but I never got to ask her out on our own, no matter how much her mother hinted. I told her I enjoyed her ma and da's company and I studied for my exams the rest of the week anyway. Things were getting dangerous – I'd stayed the night in their house a couple of times and she'd bought me a poofy identity bracelet for my birthday – when Daddy came to the rescue.

How would you like to move to Rolls Royce?" he asked me one night when I dropped into his local to have a pint before going to my Friday night ordeal.

"My time's no' out yet," I said, beginning to get angry with him for not knowing that.

"They would still take you on," he said. "A good apprentice can go anywhere if he knows the right people. It's either that or get digs here or travelling to your work from East Kilbride every day, it's up to you."

I started to ask him what he meant…

"I've put in for a transfer to the East Kilbride branch, they're taking on skilled men and it'll make us eligible for a house there. We need to get a house out of Govan, away from that railway yard, for when your sister comes out of that place." Maggie had just gone into the sanatorium with TB (another nigger away).

"What does Mammy think?" I asked to give me time to work out what would be the best thing for me.

"I'm telling her tonight," he said and I noted the 'telling' instead of asking. I knew she would, as always, do as he decided, so there was no real question.

They were leaving the Wine Alley. He was giving me the chance of going but he was not going to coax. Just when I was beginning to enjoy number sixteen, with a room and a bed to myself, he wanted to move again and to a 'new town' hundreds of miles away from Ibrox and the dancing. Still it could have its good points for me.

If Rolls Royce would take me and let me serve out my time with them – they were a much bigger firm than Dobie's – it could help me up the ladder a bit quicker. And I wouldn't need to keep in with auld Jimmie Riddock, or his daughter. There would definitely be no wedding, but I would make sure she got plenty of what she wanted before I let her down 'gently'.

"I think it's a great idea," I said. "What do I do to change my job? Will it take long?"

That was it decided. I convinced myself that it wasn't far to come to Ibrox or the dancing. There would be plenty of buses and anyway I would be able to get a wee car.

I suppose I should have felt bad about what I did that night after the club, but I've never been one of those people that think that men are always the bastards. Some women just about beg for sex. They torment you and let you do things to them and when you take over and 'go too far', they greet and blame you. It was like that wi' Sadie.

The first time we did it was that night, in her own, wee, pink and white, virgin's bedroom – although that was a kid-on for a start. I usually slept in their spare room (something the Wallace family never had) and once Jimmie and Flora were in bed, I just slipped into hers, in more ways than one. She was easier than shoplifting in Woolworths! She did everything I told her to and more. In a way I was sorry it was not going to last long. For the next week or two it was like filling your guts with your favourite sweeties, until the thought of them makes you boak. Jimmy and Flora knew what was going on. They made these horrible coy jokes about squeaky beds and 'too much bed no' enough sleep', when I was late for work. They thought I was hooked.

The day after I got word of my new job with Rolls Royce, I did a thing that some people would think was pretty lousy. I told all the lads on the shopfloor I'd fucked the foreman's daughter and she loved her hole better than any lassie I'd ever met.

He just couldn't figure it out when, one after the other of them, asked after his daughter.

"Ye must be havin' to beat the lads off wi' a stick?"

"She'll give ye braw, grand weans." Were some of the leery remarks that were made during the day but he never twigged although he knew something was going on.

It was nearly lousing time when he came charging up to my bench, like an old wifie at the C & A sales. "What's going on?" he gritted. "They've just told me you've handed in your notice. Are ye goin' daft, or what? Does our Sadie know about this?"

"What's it to do with your Sadie?" I smirked, giving a dirty wink behind his back to the other lads who had stopped cleaning up to listen.

He looked stuck for words for a minute and he moved closer when he realised it was a public conversation.

"You know fine well what it has to do with our Sadie," he whispered wetly into my face. "You're practically married to her. Her ma's talking about when the wedding will be. I think she deserves to know if you're chucking in a perfectly good job before your time is served. You'll need to be a bit more responsible when you're a married man. Ye cannae just chuck up your job when it comes up yer hump. Have you had a fa' oot wi' somebody? You want to watch that temper o' yours."

He stopped for a breath and I plunged right in, enjoying myself as if I was diving from the high board at the baths.

"One," I counted on my fingers. "I'm not marrying anybody, it certainly wouldn't be your daughter. Two, I've got a great job to go to, better pay, better conditions. Three, I've no' fell out wi' anybody, no yet anyway, bit I'll fall out wi' you if you don't sling your hook and give me peace.

I nearly felt sorry for him, but he looked too funny with his mouth hanging open and his eyes looking as if he was going to greet, like a wee boy that's lost his best marble. I had to admire him when he tried to grab my throat, but I didn't put up much of a fight. A couple of his pals bustled him away as the work's hooter sounded out like a herald's trumpet.

One thing I wasn't looking forward to was working my week's notice, but when the management heard about the row between Jimmie and me, they called me in and gave me a week's wages in lieu.

So that was it. I was ready to leave the Wine Alley and take another big step on my way to 'getting to the top'. Not many people from the Wine Alley made it but I knew I would, as long as I looked after number one.

Maggie, May, wee Jay, and Billy

CHAPTER EIGHT

Sweet Dreams

Maggie's Story

The family was getting smaller. Vicky and Terry had found a room to rent and Nancy was stationed somewhere near Blackpool. I had a room and a bed to myself for the first time in my life. I started sitting there in the evenings after school, pretending it was a studio flat in London and I was a famous writer or film star, it didn't matter what, as long as it was a famous something.

When I had the house to myself I would wander around the room in my bare white scuddy, admiring the way my body was changing from being straight up and down to curving in at the waist and out at the hips. Mr breasts looked like two pink French knots, but I was really pleased with them – pushing them up and together and doing exercises that somebody's mum had said, "Develop the breast muscles and makes them firm," so that they wouldn't sag when you were older. I missed Nancy a lot, although she wrote daft, funny letters to me, all about dancing and boys. She mentioned one name quite a lot and I began to make up a romance about him.

One day I would have him as an heroic pilot who took her on exciting flights in a small plane like the one I had seen on the front of a Biggles book, with her red hair flying in the wind and his strong, manly jaw, firm below his goggles. In another he would be the son of some lord or other, maybe even royalty, who was keeping his identity secret for some reason I hadn't worked out yet, or he was an heroic young doctor who miraculously patched up the terribly wounded pilots who were brought into his operating theatre where Nancy was his assistant.

I read everything and anything so I had plenty of romantic ideas to play with. The life I had created inside my head for Nancy was more real to me at times than what was going on in Wine Alley.

I was twelve; I had had my first period; my breasts were beginning to blossom, although still no bigger than spider's ankles; I had found that boys liked me; I was at the big school; and Billy was no longer my best pal, in fact I hardly saw him. He had been replaced by my 'best pals' Katie and Isa – although we still had a few good adventures together.

We sometimes went exploring on Sunday mornings, when everyone thought we had gone to Sunday school, which we seldom did unless there was an outing or a party coming up. Mammy gave us tuppence each for the plate, which usually went on health salts or swizzles, which we guzzled as we wandered through parks or back courts.

It was in a back court just a couple of streets away from Kellas Street that something happened that still loosens my bowels when I think about it.

We were playing a game we had made up where one of us went in one end of the air raid shelter and one went in the other, we would pass in the middle and come out at opposite ends. The thing was, it was pitch dark once you got right in and you had to feel your way along the wall to find your way out the other end. We would make creepy noises to try to scare one another and usually came running out white-faced and trying not to piss ourselves with terrified laughter. This particular shelter was unexplored territory to us and it seemed even darker than usual.

Billy decided to play a really horrible trick on me. When I thought that he was making his way through the shelter at the opposite end from me, so that we would pass in the middle, he was actually creeping along behind me, making soft snuffly noises and scuffing his feet, as the hooded monk in his comic book did. I was having a heart attack even when I knew it was him behind me, because he couldn't stop a giggle getting out and I scraped my elbow on the rough brickwork as I tried to hurry to the opening – I meant to go through and wait to pounce on him and get my revenge, but without warning I tripped over something and fell full length.

The stench was disgusting, worse than a dry lavatory.

I leapt up and stood on Billy's instep, he was so close behind me. He was doing his maniacal laugh but it stopped when he sensed that I was really scared.

"There's something here on the floor," I whispered, pressing back against the wall which felt slimy and cold against my back. It didn't seem such a good game after all.

"God, what's that smell?" Billy whispered back. "Do you think it's a body?"

That just about finished me. I had been lying on the thing. I suddenly remembered the story of the woman coming out of a haunted house with her hair turned completely white.

"We need to pass it to get through the opening, or turn back. What do you think?" I asked, not wanting to do any of them. I had never been so cold and the smell was choking me.

"I've got a couple of matches I stole from Roddy's fag tin, but I've nothing to strike them on," Billy answered. I felt my face go hot as I realised we were holding hands.

"Strike one on the wall, stupid," I said, pulling my hand away. He tried three times before we actually got a flame.

"Hold it down here," I said. "Just at my feet. I definitely fell over something."

The shape of the body could be seen clearly, although it was shapeless because of the long coat that covered it from head to broken old boots, from which a toe stuck out (I hated bare feet ever after).

"I'm not passing it," Billy choked. "It could grab our legs. Come on, we'll go back and tell somebody. Run!" And, like something out of the silent movies, we turned and bumped into one another before taking off like a spark from a log. When we had stopped running and I was able to get my breath back, without making whooping noises, I said:

"We should really go to the police, but Mammy'll kill us for going into that shelter. She warned us to keep out of those places, didn't she?"

"I'm not going to no police station!" Billy said. He, like all the lads in Wine Alley, saw the 'polis' as the enemy. One of their favourite games was shouting "Funny polis," from a hiding place in the close and watching the poor, blue soul try to find where the insult was coming from.

"We'll need to tell somebody," I said. "Maybe there's been a murder…" I nearly cut a chunk out of his arm with my nails as I thought aloud:

"Suppose the murderer was watching us and he tracks us down like dogs."

He looked a bit scared too and gave his manic laugh. "You're crazy," he laughed. "That only happens in books. It's likely some old wino that fell asleep and died of the cold. His face was probably eaten away by rats. We'll tell James Hood and maybe he could get his dad to go and look. He might even know about it. He's supposed to be a crook, isn't he?"

The upshot of this was that James Hood and about a dozen other boys from the street made us lead them back to the shelter on the Monday after school. There was no body and they chased us through the back closes, thinking we had played a joke on them, but I can still see that big, dirty, grey toe in my dreams – if I eat too much toasted cheese.

Another of our adventures was to do with the MacRoberts family, who had occupied the house before us. From what we were told by our pals in the street, one of the family, a girl called Mattie, had died from consumption when she was fourteen and another, a young man, Andy, a bad lot, had disappeared after getting at least three girls in the family way. Of course we believed that Andy MacRoberts had been murdered and now we had been given an idea how the body could have been got rid of. There were dozens of old air raid shelters all over Glasgow, ideal places for bodies to be left to rot.

Then we found the murder weapon.

We were searching in the cupboard, just outside the lavatory door, for our Christmas presents which we knew Mammy had hidden somewhere.

"I've found something," Billy whispered as he felt about on the shelf at the top of the cupboard. I was giving him a punty up to reach it and my knees were beginning to give way. "I don't think it's a present," he said. "It feels like a sharp knife."

"You stop that!" I whispered, thinking he was trying to scare me.

The next thing, just as Billy slid off my back onto the floor: "Come out of there you two!" it was Vicky's voice. She was watching us and wee Jay while Mammy went to the court with

Conn and Roddy for stealing bales of cotton wool out of a railway carriage (That's another story).

"You were told not to look for your presents," she said through angry teeth. "I'm going to teach you a lesson. I'll lock you in."

Billy just laughed madly as we heard the key turning in the lock, but I totally lost my reason and began screaming and battering the door. It was as dark as Dracula's cloak in there and only two feet square. And Billy had found a long sharp knife.

Edgar Alan Poe could not have thought up a more horrible outcome than those flashing through my mind. I kicked and thudded on the door, drowning out everything but my own terror.

"Stop battering the door. I can't get the key in." Vicky sounded a wee bit less terrified than me. She told us later that my battering had somehow twisted the lock and for a few seconds the key would not go in and then it did and would not turn. She was sure we would die of suffocation and it would be her fault. Like all mechanical things, the lock had a wicked mind of its own and just when I was sinking to my knees in a faint, the key suddenly worked and I fell out at my big sister's feet, followed by a grinning Billy, holding a rusty, murderous looking bayonet.

Vicky denied that she had believed, just for a second, that Billy had gone mad and killed me, but the look on her face gave her away. She skelped me once on the jaw and ran off into the living room in tears.

The bayonet, with its crustaceans of rust (or blood) was like a magic talisman to our imaginations. We hid it at the bottom of a drawer in my room, taking it out when it was safe, to feel the point and generally admire it. It was only a piece of old metal, but to us it had a history of bloody murder and we were sure it must have belonged to MacRoberts.

Yet the secret was too good to keep to ourselves. We told Conn and Roddy, taking it to their room when Mammy was busy ironing. It was worth giving up our secret to see the looks on their faces.

"That's definitely blood on it," Roddy said. "Rust would not be a red as that." I felt like asking him what he knew about it but I didn't want to spoil the feeling of being partners with my, usually distant, big brothers in an important conspiracy. They usually didn't even acknowledge us if they saw us in the street and Roddy warned me never to tell anyone at the 'big school' that I was his sister, or he would kill me. Big families are like that. Each member being a source of embarrassment to the others.

Billy and I were convinced that MacRoberts was dead and probably haunted the house looking for his murder weapon (or maybe he was not the murderer but the murdered) whereas Conn and Roddy thought he was alive and would come back looking for his weapon, probably when Billy and I were alone in the house.

"You better be careful," Conn said. "He could hide in the back close and grab you and nobody would be able to help you."

MacRoberts became nearly a member of the family. If there was a strange noise in the house, it was MacRoberts' ghost. An unfamiliar knock on the door or footsteps on the stairs was 'MacRoberts coming looking for you'.

*

At the same time this was going on, the main topic among me and my school pals was sex – well what we imagined sex would be like – and the combination caused me to have my first wet dream (although I didn't know what it was at the time).

We had just started the reproduction section in our biology books – no we hadn't really – one of the class had flipped ahead when she was bored listening to the teacher going on about photosynthesis, with which she sprayed the first row regularly – and found a diagram of two frogs, apparently stuck together. She held it up to the class while the teacher was writing on the blackboard for us to copy while she got on with her knitting. We all flipped pages eagerly, apart from the two swots who kept their eyes on the board, giving themselves away as having had a quick peek by going as scarlet as a Santa costume.

Most of us had a kind of idea what men and women did to one another, ranging from the tongue being very dangerous if it was put down the throat – some swore this was how you got pregnant – to the enormity of men's willies and how much stuff came out of them and where, exactly, they put them when they were 'doing it' and why men went mad for girls with big breasts – mine were boosted by hankies: in fact we were amazingly ignorant.

The school nurse had told us how to be hygienic when we had our periods, but not the reason for them and when asked about how babies were made, replied "You'll find out all about that soon enough. Keep yourself to yourself until you're married," which drove us mad with curiosity. There was one girl in Primary seven who said she knew all about it and I believe she did, but all she would say was that it was bad and disgusting and she didn't want to talk about it.

The frog diagram, two spongy-like creatures stuck together, with an ugly grin on the face of the one on top and a look of pain on the other (the man who drew it must have had a disgusting sex life) changed my mind about a lot of things. The stories in 'My Weekly' became lies; men acquired a menace which made me boak yet shiver; my dreams gained several new dimensions and I could not look at the baby frogs that Billy brought home from the pond in Elder Park, without blushing.

How MacRoberts, his bayonet and frogs came together (Literally) in one dream would probably have fascinated Freud, but it knocked me right off my perch for a while. I was scared to go to sleep at night and I couldn't even tell my best pal, Isa Biggam, about it, well not at first.

I was sitting in the back close. Helen Ranachan was there and she was holding the leg of her shorts open and looking up between her legs and crying, "It's no there mammy, it's no there. I must be a lassie." Billy was standing laughing at her and bouncing a ball off her head.

"Don't dae that," I said. "Or MacRoberts will stick his bayonet in ye. He likes big, fat frogs." The scene changed – the way they do in dreams – and I was lying on the bench in the science lab. The class were all around me, staring at something I couldn't see at the back of my head. I looked down at my breasts and there were two fat frogs on each one – doing it – I tried to knock them off but MacRoberts, who had appeared out of nowhere and looked like my form teacher, held my hands and I felt him pull my legs open and he started to climb on top of me. I couldn't push him off – something was happening – I was peeing myself but it was better than any pee I'd ever had – I wanted to laugh and cry at the same time – then it all disappeared and I could see the street light shining on the dresser in my room.

I sat up and felt between my legs. I was wet, but it wasn't pee – it didn't feel like pee and it didn't smell like pee. MacRoberts, with the help of a couple of frogs had given me my first experience of sex.

Because of where we grew up, everybody assumed that we were hard little nuts who knew it all, that's not how it was. We were much younger and softer; much more in the dark and more vulnerable than our hard little faces conveyed. Everything we knew about sex was rehashed from overheard conversations or misinterpreted from biology books. Our mothers mostly hinted at dark things awaiting us in life and generally made us feel revulsion for our own bodies.

Adolescence brings a certain amount of madness with it, and it did not miss me. As I got further into my twelfth year, I became more of an oddity. I'm a place like Wine Alley, this did not go unremarked, especially by the close mouth crows.

"Your Maggie's a funny, wee thing," Mrs Ranachan remarked to Mammy as I walked up the close with my two best pals, Isa Biggam and Katie Fernie. "Whit's she goat on her heid?"

The stupid old bitch obviously did not know that all the big film stars, Rita Hayworth, Lana Turner, Hedy Lamarr, were all wearing bandanas round their hair, tied loose in a bow just below the ear. I had borrowed one of Nancy's chiffon scarves and copied the style. I thought I looked really grown up and sophisticated. Who cared what a woman, weighing twenty stone, thought?

Isa, Katie and me were really close pals. We were in love with the same film heroes, but they were not as important to us as the several boys in the school that we had our sights set on – although we never had the courage to speak to any of them. Fantasy was our thing. It was what we lived on.

Isa was in love with two boys in the fifth year; I was in love with one boy and an English teacher and Katie loved the same people as us plus two of her own. Isa and I were little scarecrows with pretty faces and sharp minds. Katie was a bouncy dumpling with a red. shiny face from which her hated glasses constantly slipped. She had a perfect white smile and a less sharp mind than Isa's and a lot less sharp than mine.

One of the signs of my madness, was delusions of grandeur, which caused us to have 'tea parties'. Sometimes I would ask several girls from my class but mostly it was just Isa and Katie and me, sitting in the middle room with our cups of tea and packet of chocolate mallows. That was the reality!

In my mind I was 'Emma' or 'Elizabeth Bennet', serving tea to other young ladies like myself. I have never got over my first experience of reading Jane Austen and Mr Darcy would have been welcome to take MacRoberts place in my wet dreams, but he never did, no matter how I tried.

We took turn about giving these little 'soirees'. Isa provided the most excitement because we were never sure what would happen in her coup of a house. I only ever saw her mother twice. She worked in the model lodging house down by the docks and seemed to spend most of her time there. She sent Isa and me there once to get tea coupons off the old men that lived there. I never thought what she gave in return, but they seemed happy with the arrangement and gave us sixpence each into the bargain.

My visits to Isa's house were a mixture of amazement, disgust and excitement. The kitchen, which was the first room I saw, was like a lumber room, with clothes piled on most surfaces, so that it was impossible to distinguish one piece of furniture from another. There was always a pot of tea stewing on the ancient black range and an overcrowded fly-paper hanging in the window above the sink, which always had a pile of clean dishes left to drain dry. (They always seemed like the same dishes to me but I guessed they couldn't be).

On my first visit, three things happened to brighten my little girl world.

"Sit down while I get ready," Isa said, pointing to a pile of what appeared to be rags by the side of the range. "Shift that lot. They need to be ironed anyway," she said and I move as much of the bundle as I could lift to the top of another bundle in the middle of the room, which seemed to conceal a table.

The sensation that followed was that feeling of being under attack you get when someone pulls a seat from under you – there was not seat in the chair! It was just a frame and, as I sat, my arse hit the floor and my legs shot in the air, showing my bottle-green school knickers to the world at large: two boys, one a small specky creature layered in dirt and snotters, and the other tall, slim and with the looks of a young Alan Ladd, about eighteen.

How can you fall in love when you're bent double, jammed into a position which shows shameful knickers to the best looking boy you've ever seen, with an ugly, wee gremlin pointing and laughing at you and your best pal saying "I meant to tell you about that chair," when you know she didn't?

It was easy. I was in love with Isa Biggam's brother. His name was Malcolm and he was an apprentice fitter in the shipyard at the opposite side of the Old Govan Road from the Biggam's top storey tenement. He was 'triff' (that was our word for cool I suppose). He walked over to me, grabbed my arm and yanked me out of the chair, like pulling a whelk out of its shell and my backside made something like the same plopping noise as it was released. I stood with my flaming face pressed against his white shirt, liking his lifebuoy toilet smell, for about sixty seconds before he led me to a chair with a seat and sat me down, laughing and saying, "You've got to watch where you sit in this house. What's your name, Isa's pal?"

I told him my name, feeling about three years old and dying for a pee.

"Maggie," he said. "I'll call you Mags for short. OK?"

I don't know if he knew how he made me feel – that Malcolm Biggam – if he was in when I went to Isa's he would creep up on me and grab we round the waist; sometimes higher, or chase me round the room until I gave in and got tickled mercilessly, or pull my hair and frighten me with dead spiders. I don't know if he knew I was in love with him, but I was.

When he went away to England to work, I sat and gazed out of the window every night for a week, letting the tears roll down my cheeks, like Olivia de Haviland in 'The Heiress', I couldn't tell Isa I was in love with her brother. We would both have died of embarrassment. To tell anyone in the family would have meant providing material for being kidded for the rest of my life, so I sat there, enjoying every minute of my broken heart.

The other thing that happened on that first visit was I met the Biggam cat, Decky (because it had been delicate as a kitten) and I saw Isa's bedroom. She was the only girl in the family so she had a room of her own – and what a room!

The meeting with Decky came just after Malcolm had sat me down on the safe chair. It wasn't really a meeting, more a sighting. My new position meant that I was facing a kind of kitchen cabinet affair with glass-doored cupboards at the top and a sort of sideboard at the bottom. I noticed the door on the bottom cupboard was slightly open and something seemed to moving inside it. I didn't want them to get any more laughs out of me so I said in a calm voice, "I think there is something in your cupboard, Isa."

She walked over and threw the door wide. "Decky!" she yelled. "You get out of there this minute. What are you after?" A cloud of dirty orange fur streaked past me, scattering drops of blood as it went, and out the open kitchen door, chased by Isa's brothers yelling like Indian braves.

"What has it killed?" I whispered, being certain that I was going to bring up the pie I had eaten on the school bus.

"What do you mean, killed?" Isa said. "He hasnae killed anything. It was dead already. It was the meat Mammy got for our Sunday dinner. She'll kill us if the boys don't get it back off him."

I never could ask if they got it back, or whether they ate it if they did.

Isa's bedroom was the other revelation. It was four times the size of our biggest room, with an enormous bed in a recess, behind flowery, lacy curtains that reminded me of Scarlett O'Hara's bedroom in 'Gone with the Wind'. There was a high, old-fashioned fireplace and a ceiling so tall you could hardly see it. How could this palace be just across the lobby from that dangerous kitchen?

It had other wonderful things, like a great bay window, from which you could actually see men working on the decks of great ships in the dry docks: an ottoman; a wardrobe with a full length mirror for a door (I had never seen myself as a whole figure before) and pictures on the walls and a dressing table and a stool, wearing the same flouncy dress as the bed recess.

I don't know what I loved most, Isa, her brother or her bedroom but I felt somehow nourished by the whole experience – like the feeling you get after a really good big feed of your favourite food.

My other best pal was Katie, Katie Fernie. My brother used to sing to her, KKK Katie.

*

She pretended to be outraged when they sang it but we knew she loved it. She had this big crush on Conn and Roddy, who we thought of as really 'groovy'.

Mind you we had crushes on a lot of people, mostly boys but one woman teacher was the subject of some of our fantasies. We discovered that she went to watch the school football matches with her boyfriend, so we made a point of going too: we were in love with half the team anyway!

"Did you see the way he kept his arm round her all through the match?" Katie nudged me in the ribs. "I bet they're doing it all the time. He looks as if he wants to take a bite out of her. God, I feel really funny when I look at them. I wish it was me!"

Isa nudged me on the other side and gave me her look that reminded me of Madame DeFarge in our history books – wicked and gloating. "Him or her?" she asked.

"What do you mean?" asked Katie, knowing fine well.

"Who do you wish you were?" Isa said, nudging me again. "Him or her?"

"Dirty pigs," Katie glared and pretended to concentrate on the game.

It was always like this with the three of us. When it was just Isa and me we talked about Katie, about her big, matronly bust, always disguised under a hand knitted school grey cardigan; about the way she broke out in a sweat and blushed to fainting point if a male spoke to her; about the greasy spots on her forehead and her glasses, which she had to wear all the time, and about the way she always told us when she had her period as if it was the most interesting event of the year.

When it was just me and Katie, we talked about Isa, about her skinniness; her scruffy looking clothes; the way she swaggered when she walked and made fun of everybody and most of all her family, who Katie regarded as dangerous aliens.

It never occurred to me that when it was just Isa and Katie, they would talk about me. It was never just the two of them – to be friends they had to have me. I was like a bridge between them, a kind of extension lead, through which they could communicate. They never went out with one another without me, although I went with one or the other or both.

Who can explain the workings of a friendship involving three adolescent girls? Neither of them lived in Wine Alley but they were part of my life there. They displaced Billy as my best pal. He was till at the other side of the childhood river, in primary school (when he bothered to go). I had crossed over to the big school, where growing up began and there was so much we could talk about.

*

Daddy was back from Singapore. He had brought a great load of stuff which was unobtainable in the shops – tinned fruits and meats; chocolate and tins of cigarettes; a bottle of brandy and a bottle of whisky – some of these could be got but only rarely and on ration. The chocolate was still on ration as far as we were concerned because Mammy made sure we didn't make pigs of ourselves by dividing one bar between us on Friday nights.

It was his generosity with his booty which caused a major drama at number sixteen, better than anything we saw at the ABC minors.

It was Friday night, Billy and I had just been called in from the street game of rounders; Conn and Roddy were playing battleships (we were all behaving like children out of a book, because the chocolate had not been handed out yet); Vicky was knitting some large, shapeless, hairy thing; Mammy was sitting with a clean, shiny 'ready for bed' wee Jay on her lap and Daddy was studying the 'Radio Times' crossword.

We heard the front door open, but we assumed it was Big Terry coming to carry Vicky's washing home for her, she only had a tiny sink in their house.

It was Mamie Wilson, of the hairy face and toothless mouth.

The living room door was thrown open and hit Daddy's chair, making him drop his pencil. She stood there, clutching two tins of fruit, a packet of chocolate bars and a tin of Woodbines to her chest. I noticed that her hands were covered with white hairs too. She sprayed us with her words. The first were directed at Daddy who kept his eyes on his crossword.

"You can have these back. We don't need anything fae you or your family." With that she flung the tins and stuff down on the table, scattering Conn and Roddy's game. Their faces were bright red and they stared at each other as if their eyes were joined by string. I suddenly thought (please don't laugh). Then she turned her great flower bulk on Vicky, who had dropped a whole row of stitches. I could see them hanging off the needle like a broken corkscrew.

"As for you madam! Cheating a bloke into marrying you by telling him you were taking the faith! A havenae got a pucking word bad enough for you in my stomach. Buying him new suits and the rest." She leaned forward until her face was almost touching Vicky's, "You m'lady, can always say you bought your man. Ye bought Terry Wilson."

She turned and poured herself from the room like rancid fat from a chip pan and left us all like one of those tableau you used to see in furniture shop windows.

Daddy was first to speak. "Well now you know," he said. "You should have saved up and bought yourself a better one. Divide up that chocolate between ye. I was only being neighbourly but she took it the wrong way." He went back to his crossword and filled in several clues, as if the answers had just come to him.

Vicky threw her knitting down and rushed out of the room. After a while we heard voices followed by the front door shutting. She must have waited for Big Terry at the door, not wanting him to come in and be laughed at by us.

Conn and Roddy returned to their game, which seemed to be everlasting and could be taken up at any time. Billy and I were chased off to bed but I was happy. I had witnessed a real family drama; I had a whole half of a bar of chocolate to eat and Mammy's 'People's Friend' to read. Bliss was mine.

CHAPTER NINE

More Maggie

You're the end of rainbow

At Sunday school, which Billy and I were meant to attend every week, we were always told to pray for 'children less fortunate than ourselves' and it always made me feel brimming over with goodness and kindness when I did so. Although we usually spent most of our 'collection' on sweeties or chipped fruit, sometimes I polished my best halo and put a penny in the envelope for the 'black babies'. Feeling that it was best to keep in with God to some extent, just in case there was a heaven. It never occurred to us that we were 'less fortunate' because a lot of our pals in Kellas Street were the same – getting hand-me-downs or second-hand stuff from the rag store down the road. Funnily enough, most of the family remember our days living in Wine Alley as a happy time – apart from Vicky.

I don't say I liked the horrible itchy chilblains, like shiny paint blisters that blossomed on my heels every winter – because my shoes were too big – and drove me mad, so that I scratched them until they became infected and changed to a pale yellow colour, before bursting in excruciating pain – which at least brought relief from the itching – and grew nice scabs to pick, but they were not the worst thing we had to put up with – no, that was the hand-me-downs. What most adults don't understand about children is that they would rather be tortured with the implements pictured in the Primary 5 history book – thumbscrews, the rack – than be embarrassed in front of their class.

Billy and I both wore hand-me-downs. I remember one pair of trousers he had that Mammy had cut down from a pair she had got from Mrs Freckle. They had belonged to her eldest son, who had grown out of them. He was a chubby, fourteen-year-old (Billy was only nine and wiry but skinny). When the trousers were, 'made to fit', the legs were indecently wide and the button fly started somewhere around his knees. There was enough material in the seat of the pants for him to carry his books in if he had wanted to. He bunched it together and Mammy stuck a safety pin in the waist band to hold them up. The result was this figure – which presented much fun to his tormentors – of a lower half wrapped in a kind of divided skirt, with the longest fly in the world and a bustle at the back. Luckily he only had to wear it a week – most of which time he and I spent hiding in the air raid shelter until it was time to return from school – when Mammy's turn at the ménage came up and she bought him a pair of grey, school flannels (still two sizes too big so that he could grow into them).

It was bad enough for Billy and I felt as embarrassed as he did, wearing the cast-offs, but it was worse for me. Appearance is always more important to a girl and despite everything – scabby heels, infested hair and BO, I was a vain person I hated the posh girls in my class but – craven coward that I was – I wanted to be one of them. In my memory they were all rosy-cheeked, with hair in plaits or bunches and wearing brand new looking pleated skirts with jumpers without holes in the elbows or gymslips with white blouses and red sashes.

I remember some of the scruffs as well, who were usually made to sit in the front row of the class, because they were stupid as well as scruffy, but that memory is not so vivid, because they were not important to me, in fact I cringed away from them with just as much horror as my posh classmates did. The only thing that saved be from totally being looked on as one of them, was my smartness.

It didn't stop the sniggers when I had to wear Nancy's 'new look coat to the school trip, because my trench coat was literally falling apart. I would have laughed myself if someone else had turned up in that coat. Nancy was tall and she had looked great in the pale green, full skirted coat, which had little flounces on the hips, but the eight inch hem Mammy had sewn in it, made it like a hooped skirt and my legs like loose threads hanging from it. I could only see the top half of myself in the mirror in the living room before I left, carrying my pieces in one of Vicky's patent handbags which I had borrowed. I looked fine. I had no bust to fill it out and the shoulder seams kept sliding down towards my elbows, but with my frizzed out hair and little chiffon scarf at the neck – I looked fine.

In the gym hall, where we had to assemble to wait for the bus, there were two huge, full length mirrors on one wall. Like a pheasant preening itself in front of the men who are going to scatter its feathers to the four winds and turn it into a gourmet meal – all unaware of my own imminent destruction – I waltzed up to where my classmates were admiring themselves in the mirror. They were all wearing their Sunday best – some of them even had hats on.

I should have known the way they parted to let me through, as if I were a doctor at an accident, on a mission to save a life. But nothing could save me! There I stood, like an upside down, green, spinning top with little reddish, blue legs, like spirtles. Some of them had the decency to laugh behinds their hands, but mostly they shrieked (as only vicious little girls can do) and pointed at my eight inch hem, which now had a wavy appearance as the material became too heavy for May's stitching and it made for the ground like waves to the shore.

As soon as we got on the bus, I took the coat off and threw it up on the rack. I sat down in a window seat and gazed out as they walked past one by one, not wanting to be infected with the ridicule that stuck to me. When I felt the seat beside me sinking, my spirits rose for a second, as I thought one of my girl classmates was going to 'pal' me, despite my appearance, but sank again when I saw who had sat beside me – the class clown, Murdo McIvor! Heads turned and giggles were set free as he sat back in his seat like a king surveying his subjects and beamed around the bus, smiling and nodding to the other boys, as if he had won first prize at the fair. I stared out the window, but that was worse than facing them, it's better to be laughed at to your face than to your back.

When the bus started up, everyone wanted to float paper streamers out of the windows and I felt my stomach lurch when he stood up and reached over me to open the window. I was dying to scratch my head (I hoped Mammy's Derback soap had not left any beasts in it or he would maybe see them when he looked down at me) but his words made me forget that worry.

"Do you want some streamers to put out?" he asked, holding a bunch out to me. "You hold them out the window and I'll tie them on the catch, come on." I stood up beside him and took the streamers.

"Hey Murdo," a boy's voice yelled from behind us. "I like your girlfriend." Followed by a wolf-whistle, which others took up.

He carried on tying the streamers and then turned to face the class and thumbed his nose "Better than sitting besides you, fat boy," he said to the boy who had started the noise. "At least I won't have to wear a gas mask!" This turned the laughter away from me and I began to feel that I might enjoy the outing – as long as I left the coat on the bus.

I did enjoy it. I learned a lesson that day: If a popular person shows that they accept you, others will follow his lead. Murdo was the most popular boy in the school and some of his stardust had fallen onto me.

There were other times when I borrowed my sister's clothes which did not turn out so well. The worst of these was all tied up with Mammy's aversion to telling us anything about our bodies. We were a family of four sons and three daughters, but I had never seen another person naked and the word sex (under any of its many aliases was never mentioned in our house).

Birth was never mentioned by name, nor pregnancy. She would say, "So and so has got a new wee baby," as if it was something you bought in the baby shop.

I remember once, Conn, with all the sophistication of a fifteen-year-old, announced at the tea table. "My pal's big sister is expecting a baby," and Mammy had jumped up and started clearing away our plates before we had finished.

"That's enough of that kind of talk, Conn Wallace," she said as if he had come away with something really shocking that meant he had to be called by his full name. After that I used to feel embarrassed if I even saw a pregnant woman on the opposite side of the street. If it hadn't been for my pals I wouldn't even have known what caused the swollen bellies of the souls.

I didn't know what periods were, other than the dot that ends a sentence. I suspected there was some disgusting thing that women had to go through when they grew up, connected with the sly remarks boys made about Nanny pads and 'the curse', but I had no idea what it was. Sex education in schools was given by the school nurse and it was all to do with hygiene – how we should have a bath at least once a week (She must never have heard of back to back fires) but not at certain times of the month when we should not go to the swimming baths or wash our hair either.

The mystery was partly cleared up for me on the day I borrowed Nancy's new, silk, flowery skirt, that Daddy had sent her. It had a matching top and Vicky had got one too. I got a box of hankies, with the days of the week embroidered on them. I loved the feel of that skirt. I had to pull it right up to my oxters, tie a belt round the middle and pull my jumper down to hide the bulge. I thought I looked like a fairy in it and kept rubbing the silk against my legs.

I was wearing thick, cotton, school knickers under it and for once I was glad of them. I was walking home from school, arm in arm with my two best friends, feeling the glow of being one of the crowd, when I felt a trickling between my legs – at first I thought it was something crawling – and the group of girls walking behind us started to giggle.

"Oh Jean," one of them said, in that friendly voice young girls use when they see an opportunity for cruelty. "You must have sat on something. You've got a stain on your new dress." I twisted the skirt round, dreading what I would see. The flower pattern was blue on a white background yet, about six inches above the hem of the dress was a bright red splotch, looking like a flower which did not belong.

"Turn it round to the front and cover it with your bag," one of my friends whispered. "Do you know what it is? Didn't your mother tell you to wear a pad?"

I could only guess that the 'disgusting thing' had happened to me without my knowing. Luckily I covered it up so quickly that not many people saw it, but all I worried about was how to hide the skirt, before Nancy saw it.

I got away with it. All our dirty washing was shoved into the boiler in the kitchen and every Wednesday (our day for the clothes poles) Mammy filled it up with water and soap powder and did her washing – she didn't have time to go through it and wash delicates separately, so when Nancy next saw her skirt it would only fit my doll, but the stain was gone.

I don't know how Mammy knew the 'disgusting thing' had started but she came into the room that night, where I was sitting at the window, feeling tragic, and handed me a folded up piece of flannelette sheet, which had worn thin and was now being used for dusters and washing clothes.

"Use that until you're better," she said, not looking at me, "and put it in the outside bin when you've finished with it – not the bin in the kitchen. You'd better throw your knickers out as well, I'll get you a new pair."

I wanted her to put her arms round me and tell me it was all right, that I hadn't done something wrong, that she didn't think I was disgusting. I wanted to ask questions about this thing that was happening to me. Did it happen to her? How often did it happen? Why did it happen? My throat was sore trying to keep from crying, but she just turned and walked out of the room leaving me feeling diseased and abandoned.

I had just turned eleven.

I was so ashamed of this normal function of the female body, that for years I felt it had to be kept secret and not even talked about with my own sisters or my best friend. Some societies celebrate a girl becoming a woman; some modern families talk openly when their daughter reaches this wonderful milestone in her life, but all it brought me was guilt and despair.

The hand-me-downs continued to embarrass Billy and I while giving everyone else a good laugh. Shoes were Mammy's worst worry. Good shoes were too dear and we could wear out the cheap ones in a matter of weeks. Sand shoes were cheap and we could wear them for gym as well, as long as the teacher did not notice that you were wearing the same shoes on the gleaming floors of the gym as you had worn to walk to school. The only thing was, they let in the rain so we often squelched our way through the day.

Mrs Miller, a kind teacher, noticed the water oozing out of my sand shoes one day when I had been sent into her class with a message from my own teacher. She noticed because her class could not help themselves laughing when I made a noise like someone paddling in a burn as I walked from the door to her desk (they were meant to be reading silently). She slammed her pointer down on the front desk and their laughter withered away in fear.

A few days after this she sent for me to come to her class at the interval. She was the kind of woman who makes you want to lay your head on her breast. She was a round, cushiony kind of woman who always wore flowery smocks over her clothes when she was teaching. Her face was round and downy, her hair was white and framing her face like a Dutch doll's and she had small rounded hands with which she patted the round bun snuggling at the back of her head. She smelled like Pears soap and Pond's face powder. If God had set out to make the opposite of Miss Dorian, he had succeeded in Mrs, Miller.

She was standing behind her high, teacher's desk when I went in, racking my brains to think why she would want me. I had been nipping one of the girls in her class, because I hated her fat legs but I didn't think she would have clyped me (not if she didn't want done!)

"It's nothing to worry about," she said, smiling and pointing to the seat beside her desk. "I want you to do an errand for me." It turned out that she had a friend, an elderly lady, who lived at the far end of Kellas Street from us and she wanted me to take a letter and some books to her.

She handed me the square parcel with the books (I supposed the letter was inside) and then brought another, quite bulky, parcel out from under the desk.

"These are for you," she said. "I hope your mother will not mind. I noticed your feet were very wet the other day and I know shoes are expensive." Her face matched mine in redness by the time she had finished speaking and I hoped this was a weird dream I was having. What a laughing stock I would be if folk knew I was wearing a teacher's cast-off shoes.

"No one will know anything about this," she said. It will be a secret between us. If anyone asks just say both parcels are for my friend, Miss Lynn."

I couldn't help myself looking down at her feet. She was wearing quite decent looking black, lace up shoes and her feet were pretty small but not as small as mine. She read my thoughts again. "They may be a wee bit big but your mother can buy insoles and you can wear thick socks. They'll be better than those sand shoes. At least your feet will be dry."

"Thank you, Miss," I said.

I delivered the books on the way home, to old Miss Lynn, a retired teacher, who gave me threepence to myself and a pat on the head. The other parcel I shoved on top of the bunker in the kitchenette. I thought I could throw it in the bin later and tell Mrs Miller that the shoes didn't fit me or even take them back and tell her my mother had told me not to take them. Of one thing I was sure, I was not going to wear them. What if somebody at school recognised them? I was just beginning to live down Nancy's flouncy coat and that was because I had put it about that I had just worn it for a laugh. I would have to hide forever in the air raid shelter if I had to wear these shoes.

I was curled up on my bed, reading the 'Maria Martin' serial in the 'Red Star Weekly', totally lost to the world of Wine Alley, when I heard Mammy shouting, "Who left this parcel on the bunker? Maggie did you leave this here? Come and shift it, whatever it is. I need the space to put out the dinner!"

She had the shoes out of the wrapping paper by the time I went through.

"Where did you get these?" she asked.

"Mrs Miller, the teacher, gave them to me," I said. "The cheek of her! She told me they would be better than sand shoes. She said they would keep my feet dry. I'm not wearing them!" I expected her to be angry at a teacher expecting me to wear her cast-offs. How could I know how desperate poverty can make you, when you have children wearing shoes out quicker than a shoe factory could replace them.

"They're a nice shoe," she said turning them round, admiring the leather soles and, horror beyond belief, Cuban heels. "She's quite right. They are better than sand shoes. Mind you, they're a bit big for you."

I smiled and held out my hand for them. "I know. Will I just take them back to her (you could give me a note) or will we throw them out?"

"We're not going to hurt the woman's feelings," she answered. "I'll get insoles for them tomorrow and you can try them on with a pair of thick socks. Beggars can't be choosers you know!"

They were all ready for me the next day when I got in from school and I had to try them on and walk up and down the living room so that Mammy could see how they looked.

"They're really smart," she said. "I bet they cost more than I could spend on a whole outfit. Your feet will be as dry as a bone in them and you'll soon get used to the heels."

Two words flashed across the screen of my mind as I looked at myself in the wardrobe mirror in the big bedroom – Minnie Mouse! Apart from being too big for me, even with insoles and thick socks, the high heels gave me a Minnie Mouse walk, with the upper half of my body seeming always to beat my backside by a short head and my skirt riding up accordingly.

Funnily enough, some of my classmates were envious of me for being allowed to wear high heels at the age of ten and a bit, but most of them laughed and pointed. Thank God they didn't know where the shoes came from or I would have been as well jumping in front of a train.

"Couldn't you just ask Granda Wallace to get me another pair of shoes?" I begged after my first day of wearing them. My ankles were sore and I had two red blisters on my heels but worst of all my pride was beaten nearly to death. Some of the boys had taken to imitating my walk. I was the star turn! The most popular entertainer in the playground without even trying!

She started clattering about, shoving things into drawers, scraping chairs on the linoleum, poking the fire and generally being agitated.

"I can't keep asking your grandpa for help," she snapped. "You didn't look after the last pair he bought you." I thought she probably hadn't paid him back, so I dropped the subject and went and changed into my sand shoes, which now seemed like Cinderella's glass slippers to me.

The shoes were soon replaced by something else for the class to laugh at (The school nurse put purple ointment on a girl's head) and my blisters burst and scabbed over, just as my pride grew a hard shell to protect it.

The authorities must have dredged some evil swamp for the school nurses of that time – those I met up with anyway. The purple ointment was only one of the tortures they used to humiliate children and I was always relieved after the monthly visit that I arrived back in the class with my 'dirty fair' hair without purple highlights.

The word in the playground was that it was called gentian violet and it was used for impetigo and scabies, that only people with dirty heads caught. I never saw any of the 'posh' weans with purple blotches. It was always the poor lot who sat in the front row – the dunces. No one would stand next to them in lines or partner them at gym and they even turned against one another, like dull, wee sparrows who peck a budgie to death because of its bright colours.

I was no different.

I remembered having scabies – during the evacuation – and I didn't want to catch them again. Years later, when I me a girl who had taken the ridicule away from me, I had forgotten her real name, but I remember we called her 'Coconut Heid'.

It was usually the 'have-nots' who were bullied by the 'haves', but sometimes the 'haves' became 'have more than anybody elses' and they became everybody's target – especially if they were clypes.

Cathy Mackay was a clipe. She also had everything that wee girls want: long blonde hair, which she wore, sometimes, in ringlets, sometimes in fat, edible plaits; long sticky-out eyelashes; lovely rosy cheeks; hundreds of box-pleated skirts and fuzzy jumpers in winter and flowery, cotton dresses, with puff sleeves, in summer and a real leather satchel …oh and the biggest, best equipped pencil case in the world! I spent hours every night before I fell asleep planning how I could get that pencil case, without being found out.

At first when she came into our class, everybody, apart from the front row lepers, wanted to be her friend. The boys showed off in front of her and the girls wanted to sit beside her. I can't remember why everybody turned against her. She was a bit of a show-off and always handed her homework in on time and she had a silly little 'plum in the mouth' voice, but I don't think it was any of those things. It seemed to start from the day she put her hand up and told the teacher that the boy behind her was pulling her pigtails and the teacher took her word for it and gave the boy, Murdo McIvor, my hero, three of the belt, crosshands.

Only a little group of the sneakiest girls spoke to her at playtime. The boys ignored her and the rest of us kept pushing into her accidentally. I got a really good nip at the top of her leg when she was walking up the stairs in front of me and Miss Dorian gave her a shake for making a noise in the lines. We were meant to enter and leave the school silently, marching in time to stirring tunes played on an ancient upright piano by Tarzan, the music teacher.

If she had learned her lesson then – what happens to clypes – I don't think we would have turned on her the way we did, but she seemed to have something wrong with her which made her hand shoot up when she saw anyone breaking the rules.

"Please sir, Johnny's chewing."

"Please sir, Mary's trying to copy from me."

"Please sir, Maggie Wallace nipped me."

It was as if her arm was operated by a puppet master. She just couldn't help herself. What made it worse, even the teacher, Mr Zimmer, was beginning to turn against her. At first he punished everyone she pointed her little, manicured finger at but then he began to try to ignore her whines and finally said to her, trying to be kind but sounding as if it were a big effort.

"Come along now Cathy, get on with your work, it's not nice to be always telling tales on your classmates. Is it?"

She burst into tears! Clyping was the worst thing anyone could do in our world. Second was greeting and she did both practically at the same time. It was after we heard her mother – toffee nosed bitch – had been up to the headmaster about Mr Zimmer that we (well I suppose it was my idea) decided to take revenge on her.

The campaign began on a Monday, at the morning interval. She was standing on her own, just inside the main door, eating a lovely rosy apple (I'd never had a whole apple to myself). Just as she was about to take a bite, I walked up and hit her hand so that the apple hit her on the face, before flying out of her hand and onto the floor, where one of my pals kicked it to another and a game of kickabout went on until there was none of it left. She made a run for the stairs, crying like a baby, but I caught hold of one of her plaits (tied with red, satin ribbon that day) and pulled her back and outside to the playground, to the manic cheers of weans who had become savages.

We made a circle round her like Hollywood's idea of an Indian war party and danced around singing:

Tell-tale Tit
Your tongue will be split
An' a' the people in the town
Will have a wee bit

The circle was closing in on her and we were spitting our song into her face. I felt as if I was the top person in the world and she was in my power. I wanted to pull her pigtails off and nip her all over. God knows what would have happened if Mrs Miller, who was on playground duty, hadn't appeared round the corner and blew her whistle. We answered to the shrill sound, like sheep with the dog at our heels and made straight lines in front of the door.

Cathy Mackay stood there, her pigtail unravelled, red ribbons clutched in her hands; lovely rosy cheeks drowning in snotters and tears; ready to clype again.

I felt no pity for her.

She did not return to class after playtime and at the dinner interval we heard that her mother had come up to the school and taken her home.

She could only remember six names and of course mine and Murdo's were among them. The headmaster came and took us out of class in the afternoon. I wasn't frightened. I was wetting my knickers but it was with a kind of mad joy – not fear.

Mr Williams, the Head, who looked like a weedy Clark Kent, belted all of us in a row, his heels rising up as his arm came down and the three pronged belt swished and smacked onto our crossed hands.

"Now get out of my sight," he said when he reached the end of the row. Everyone was crying except Murdo and me, "and let me hear no more about bullying."

We had an hour to sit in class, trying to write the composition Mr Zimmer had set us on bullying. As I forced my swollen hand to hold the pencil and write the usual stuff about bullying being cowardly etc etc, I was forming a plan for revenge.

We knew Cathy lived in one of the 'bought' houses, two streets sway from the school and it was to there that I led my band of avengers at four o'clock. I was not quite sure what I intended to do when we got there, only that we were going to make her sorry for clyping on us (my hand was still throbbing).

There were about twenty of us to start with, but that dwindled to ten when we reached unfamiliar territory – houses with driveways and front lawns, even some with gates. Cathy's had a wrought iron gate, lying open and rhododendron bushes in front of the bay windows, through which we could see her white, terrified face before she went to get her mother.

We stood there chanting our song about what happens to tell-tales, feeling that something more vicious was called for, 'to learn her a lesson'. There was a funny smell in the garden and when I saw where it came from, I knew just what to do. I threw the first bit of dung and screeched like a banshee as it spattered against the sparkling glass. It looked as if it had landed on Cathy's face and the next clod obliterated her completely. We scrabbled among the horseshit not caring that it was squelching over our shoes and sticking to our fingers. All reason had gone. We were getting our revenge on Cathy for being clean and pretty and having a better life than us, although we thought it was for being a clype.

When the front door opened and her mother stood Fthere, we just turned and ran, no one dared to defy that tall, well dressed figure, more like a teacher than a mammy.

Cathy never returned to our school.

She couldn't have given names this time, because the head just gave a long harangue against bullying at the next assembly.

We got off with it.

Bullying was a fact of life for us. We dealt with it, either bullying others or, as Billy did, just staying away from school. It was while I was out in sympathy with him that we had some of our best adventures.

CHAPTER TEN

There Ain't No Boys

John's Story

You would think open spaces, being back with your wife and family, being a hero and having money in your pocket would more than satisfy a man who had been in a German prison camp for four years, yet I was only back a year when I felt that I was in the wrong place at the wrong time and, worst of all, with the wrong people.

Every day was the same. I got up early to get the older weans to school, while May attended to the new baby; read the papers; wrote out my bookie's line for the day; wandered down to the hotel; put the line on and chatted to the locals until it was time to go back up the road for my tea. Most days I was half-scooped and May would sit nursing her wrath (as Burns said) while I tried to get the weans to like me.

It wasn't working.

Vicky and Nancy were staying with their granny Ross in Glasgow, where she had got them jobs in the fur trade – to serve their time as fur-finishers. I had made them pack in the jobs I had got them in a hotel in the next village. (I worried that these Ayrshire men wouldnae think twice about coupling any young lass and mine were two wee beauties) The two boys – Conn and Roddy were OK. They went straight out again as soon as they had finished their tea, usually to play football in the park. Sometimes I had a kick about with them and showed them the ball skills that had got me a trial for Clyde once, but I was getting fed up wi' that and usually left them after an hour or so to go back to the pub. I had everything me and the other blokes had talked about for hours during the long nights in the POW camp, but I couldn't be happy.

The wee lassie, Maggie, kept me amused, telling me about their teacher – Fuddy Duck – even demonstrating why she got her name, but even she seemed to prefer playing wi' her pals or Billy, her wee brother – and he just didn't want to know me. Ever since that night I had put him out of his mother's bed, I would catch him scowling at me from under his brows, blaming me for displacing him twice – once by my arrival home and secondly by having something to do with the presence of the new baby, which took all his mammy's time. He was nearly as unhappy as me. Probably with more reason.

When the letter arrived it sent May into a panic but I saw it as a godsend. It was from the lawyer for the Misses McWhirter, who owned the cottage we lived in. It pointed out that they had let us stay much longer than any other evacuees in the village and, although they realised we had been paying rent, they now wanted their cottage back as soon as possible. They were sure we would have no problem "Getting accommodation in your native city and we wish you all the best."

So that was that. Off I went to Glasgow to see what our 'native city' could do for a man wi' a wife and seven weans.

'Bugger all' was the answer to that question, if I'd been daft enough to listen to the wee office jerk who told me there was a long waiting list for corporation houses and we would have to wait our turn. He changed his tune when I got a wee but physical wi' him and the upshot was I could phone May with the good news that we could move into a house in a week, It was a five apartment, up one stair and the rent wouldnae skin us. I was still living on my army payout but I would soon get a job.

The new Labour government had promised full employment.

Since the first time I came home, I felt that I was moving forward in my life. The time in Ayrshire had seemed like a holiday, where everything stood still. The suspended feeling of the prison camp was still with me. I had still seemed to be waiting for something to happen. As it had been in the camp, every day was the same. It was pleasanter: there wasn't the fear of the Germans winning the war (We had no idea what would happen to us if they did), but there was no one to share the memories with. I couldn't talk to May and the weans about how it had been. How could anyone who hadn't been there understand what it was like?

This would be a 'the new beginning' all of us had talked about in that barren place.

After I had talked to May on the phone, I walked to Granny Ross's to see the lassies and tell then the news. I could have got the subway but I was choking for a pint and I needed something to sweeten the medicine of meeting the in-laws.

Their hate for me still burned in my heart. I had done the right thing when May told me she was expecting – giving up my sweetheart for her – but there was nothing they liked about me. I was an unemployed ne'er do well from the tough end of Govan and my family were all Catholics. Being captured early on in the war only added to my faults as far as they were concerned. And getting May in the family way as soon as I returned should have been a castrating offence to them.

The first thing Granny Ross said, fiddling with the wee, tight bun she always rolled her hair into with shiny hands with washing everything that could be washed, closing her thin lips with a snap after every word, was: "You might have given yourselves a bit of time before getting her expecting again, as if six wasn't enough, you must be the talk of the place. How do you expect to feed and clothe seven weans wi' the rationing and the prices?"

Not giving me time to answer – she never had – "You better stay for your tea. The lassies will be in any minute."

The smell of her home-made soup was making my teeth water. She was a bitter auld bitch but she was the best cook I ever knew.

It was funny when I told the lassies about the house. I expected the two of them to be really excited about it – coming back to live with their mammy and their brothers and sisters. Nancy was, she threw her arms around my neck and giggled, but I could see she was holding back a bit so as not to upset her granny.

"We'll be able to come and visit you a lot," she said. "It's really just down the road and Mammy will be glad to be near."

Vicky's reaction was like a smack on the mouth for me. Her face turned white and pinched up as if she was sucking something sour. "I want to stay here with my granny," she said. She let on that it would 'give you more room', but I knew that wasn't the real reason. Granny Ross had got to her and made her think she was a cut above the rest of us. I was having none of that.

Auld Granda – all five feet two of him – backed them up and said she could easy stay on with them, but I stuck my heels in and told her to be ready to come with Nancy and me to get the house ready for her mother and the other weans coming. There was no question of her staying with her granny.

I wasn't just being thrawn. I remembered how I had been brought up wi' my granny while my two wee sisters were with different aunties, when our mother had died. I hardly ever saw them and didnae even get to their funerals when they died.

No, we would stick together as a family if I had anything to do with it. Maybe we could really get to be a family, once I has a job and the weans were in new schools. These wee village schools had been no use to them. I wanted them to have everything I never had – no lack of brains, I always had plenty of them – a good education, university and all that, or if they werenae clever enough for that – a white-collar job, where you tell people what to do other than having some jumped-up bastard wi' only half your brains telling you what to do.

The army had taught me a lot about 'them and us'. I saw how, even as prisoners, officers were treated better than us. I saw how they were always in authority over us, although in camp quizzes and crosswords, I was always better than them. I hated the way their class gave them confidence, that they were superior and had to make sure the 'men' were 'kept up to scratch'. I saw how annoyed they were when I was used as an interpreter by the Gerries. I had used my schoolboy German as a stepping stone to building a good understanding of the language – better than any of the officers, who had all studied Latin and Greek (fat lot of use that was to them).

Well, I might be a bit late to see Vicky and Nancy got a good education, but I had got them into a good trade and it wasn't too late for the rest of them. The first thing was to get them into a good school. I decided that May should take them to Ibrox school, instead of the one nearest to us. It was nothing more than a ragged school, where the lowest of the low went. From Ibrox they would have a good chance of going on to Belahouston, Govan High or even Hutcheson Grammar for wee Maggie and Alan Glenn's for the boys.

Living in Wine Alley was not going to keep them back. It was only going to be temporary, we wouldn't be there forever. I would make sure they didn't get involved wi' any o' the toerags around there, particularly the Catholics.

That would be the first thing.

That few days wi' my two daughters were some of my best ever and I think they enjoyed it too. We scrubbed the place, set out the utility furniture they picked, put up the curtains Granny Ross gave us and laughed a lot. Vicky forgot all about wanting to stay with her granny and for the first time since I came home, I felt that I really was home. We ate fish suppers out of the paper and made plans for 'doing up' the house once we had settled in. The auld wife across the landing was really good, bringing us cups of tea and cleaning stuff and telling us about the other folks in the close.

Vicky and Nancy reckoned she was the ugliest person they'd ever seen but she 'has a good heart' they decided, trying not to laugh when I stuck out my tongue at her behind her back.

The night before I was going to help May to bring the rest of them to their new home, I took mugs of cocoa (thanks to Granny Ross) and biscuits to them once they were in bed and we had a long talk about the future.

"This is a fine house," I said, It'll do us until we get something better, wi' a room for each of you and a back and front garden. I know you liked staying wi' your granny but it's no' right for a family to be split up." Vicky kept her eyes down, as if there was something fascinating in the cocoa. "Just you give me time and your granny will want to come and stay with us, our house will be that posh." They giggled and cooried into one another, like wee kittens in their basket and I felt like greeting' I was that happy that they were my daughters. This was more like the scenes me and my mates had pictured when we were in Stalag B.

"There's one or two things I want you to remember." I felt that I had to let them see that what I had to say next was very serious. So I took one each of their hands – Vicky's was freezing cold and Nancy's was warm and moist – and held them as I explained: "This is a big house and we're a big family, too big for your mammy to look after on her own, We'll need to muck in and help, especially you two." They both nodded, but Vicky withdrew her hand and put it under the covers,

"The other thing I want you to remember, and it's even more important," I said. "Is that you're to have nothing to do wi' the people in the street – oh don't be unfriendly! Say hello and that, but don't get friendly with them. You're a different class fae these people. This is only gonnae be your home for a wee while. Don't get pally wi' the lasses and for God's sake don't go out wi' any of the blokes. Remember that. They're no good enough for you. You're a different class."

Vicky was nearly nodding her head off in agreement but Nancy looked mixed up and red in the face.

"Will they no' think we're snobs?" she asked.

"Better they think that than ending up married tae one of them!" I laughed to cheer her up, but she still looked a bit worried when I said goodnight and put out the light.

*

It was good at first: distempering the rooms: teaching the boys to play games I had learned, God know when; coming in at night to a good tea; asking them how they were doing at school and trying the break down the wall of strangeness between us.

It was working with Nancy, Conn, Roddy and Maggie. Nancy was so easy-going about life in general that she just accepted that I was back and was glad I had got them a new house – my only worry about her was that she couldn't help enjoying the attention she got from the local corner boys, but I had no fear that she would ever go out with any of them; she just liked the whistling and flirting like any lassie her age would.

Anyway, if they tried to go further than whistling, I would tear their heads off then. And they knew that. People in Govan hadn't forgotten me.

Conn and Roddy were entirely different natures, but they were great pals with each other and ever since I had sorted out the fight they had had in the street when we had just arrived, they were quite pally wi' their wee daddy. I'd managed to wangle Conn a good apprenticeship and Roddy's school reports were second to none. I felt I was really getting somewhere with these three.

Vicky was different, yet she remembered me better than any of them: maybe that was the trouble. She remembered the bad times, when I'd rolled home drunk – with no money in my pockets – and her mammy had been in tears – I kept hoping she would remember the good times too, but I always felt that I was being expected to say sorry to her and I didn't like that. Still, in a way, she was my favourite and I wondered how her life would have been if she'd had better chances than I could give her. The sad thing was she always seemed dissatisfied. May was convinced that she hated her wee brothers and sisters and I began to believe her. When I tried to have a talk to her about being so hard on them: "They're only weans," I said, after she had caught Billy and Maggie playing with her makeup.

"You don't have to put up with them!" she said. "They're nearly always in bed when you get in from the pub." She had put me on the penitents stool again. I was losing Vicky and I didn't know what to do about it.

Maggie, like Nancy, had accepted me and would tell me all her wee lassie adventures from school and tell me what books she was reading from the library. She reminded me a lot of my dead sister, Maggie, and that worried me. She had been really bright as well, but consumption got to her before she had a chance to grow up. Maggie was skinny and under-sized but according to the school doctor, she was healthy enough – just 'small for her age'.

Billy was still a problem.

If the wall Vicky had built between us was high and thick, the one he had built had barbed wire on top of it. My hands were bleeding trying to reach out to him. I could cope with being hated by an adult – but a wee boy of seven, that was really hard. He didn't want to know me and usually spent his time in his bedroom or outside if I was in the house. He had a strange way of sneering, yet being defensive when I spoke to him, which just unmanned me and I gave up.

On top of all this, there was the bloody job.

The bureau had sent me to a job as a labourer in the gasworks and I had started off with every intention of sticking it out, despite people moving away from my smell when I went on the tramcar on my way home, but two things happened to change my mind.

One was having to work with two of the most miserable bastards I had ever met – and they had cause to be miserable, as I found out soon enough. The other was something May told me that did something inside that I couldn't get over.

First of all, there were my workmates. An old fella called Denny – an Irishman, and a younger lad by the name of Eck. I noticed the queer feeling towards them from the other lads on the shift, the very first day, when we were sitting having our break. As usual there were remarks about what each of us had in our 'pieces', I had cheese and brown sauce on three slices and meat paste on the fourth, plus a couple of tea biscuits on butter. I was quite happy with that, after all, May had nine of us to feed, so I didn't expect roast beef or steak, cheese was fine.

"Bloody pink lint again," Jerry the apprentice said when he opened his poke. "My ma has nae imagination. That's the third day in a row." The other men laughed, there were six of us all together, and got stuck into their pieces after revealing what they contained I noticed that Denny and Eck didn't join in the banter and moaning but just sat quietly eating their food.

"You two must have something good," I said, winking to young Jerry. "No pink lint for you, eh?"

Denny looked up at me as if he were about to speak, but Jerry got in first. "You don't want tae know whit they're eating," he said. "Shite would be too good for them."

The others nodded their agreement and Denny and Eck got up and left the table, taking their pieces with them. Neither man spoke.

The hooter went for going back to work so I didn't get a chance to ask what was behind the bad feeling towards the two men, who seemed pretty harmless to me. It was nearly a week before I found out. I got Sandy, the foreman, along the road on the walk to the subway at the end of the day and I asked him what it was all about.

"That Denny," he snarled. "The murdering bastard murdered his wife and got away with it, so he did."

"Surely no'!" I said, letting him know that I wanted to hear the whole story.

It turned out that his wife (a lovely woman according to Sandy) had worked for years behind the bar in a pub in Govan that was a favourite wi' the working men in the area. Everybody had liked her but she wasn't interested in 'taking up wi' any of the punters, although some of them had chatted her up occasionally. She was faithful to her man, who everybody agreed was a dour, nasty piece of work, and just lived for her two kids, a lad and a lassie. Everybody knew he lifted his hand to her, by the black eyes that she tried to cover up with heavy makeup, but she always made excuses if anyone remarked on them, laughing and saying she was always bumping into things.

"She was found at the foot of the stairs – lying in the close – wi' a broken neck, one Sunday morning and he was arrested. They had to get him up oot of his bed. What made it worse, was, when he was tried, he made out she'd been a right hoor and that it could have been one of her 'fancy men' that had killed her. He got his son tae back him up in court – imagine a lad blackening his own mother's name like that, eh?"

"Bloody awful," I said, but I couldnae help thinking that there maybe was more to it than he was saying. No' many barmaids in Govan would stay pure for long!

"What about the other fella, Eck?" I asked. "What have you got against him? He seems a fine enough lad."

"Aye, fine enough," he said. "He's Denny's son, the bastard."

The whole thing gave me the creeps and when Denny was found at the foot of a forty foot ladder a couple of days later, and Eck was taken away, I decided I wanted to look for another job, but what happened next between May and I meant I didnae have to.

*

We hadn't been out together, properly, since my first night back and I felt she needed a break from the house and the weans, so I told Vicky and Nancy not to make plans for the Saturday night because I was taking their mammy out and I wanted them to stay in and watch the wee ones.

I bought her a nice new blouse so she couldn't say she had nothing to wear and the lasses promised to do her hair. She said she didnae want to go; that she had too much to do; wee Jay was teething; she didn't like leaving them to make sure the rest came in and went to bed when they were told, but that was par for the course. I knew she was really looking forward to it, so I booked tickets for a show at the Metropole and told the lasses to make sure she was ready by 6 o'clock. They were loving it – doing up her hair and lending her a skirt and jacket to go with the blouse. This was how I had pictured things. This is what families did. Once I got a better job out of that miserable place we would all be on the road.

The show was first class and May laughed at all the jokes and sung along with all the songs. I enjoyed watching her better than the show and made her blush like a wee lassie when I kissed her, right in front of the theatre crowd, as we walked arm in arm up Sauchiehall Street to the wee place I was taking her to for supper. We'd had a couple of drinks before the show and I ordered two more as soon as we got to our table.

*

For years I asked myself why I spoiled it – was it the drink? I don't know, but that night was the end of May and me and what I thought a family should be.

She started it really, when she said, in a sort of coaxing voice, as if she felt that we could at last talk, "You never tell me about anything that happened to you all these years you were away,

Johnnie. Was it all too bad to talk about, or what? Men and wives should be able to tell each other things."

"Some things were bad," I answered. "Things I'll never talk about, even to you. I just want to forget all about it. It wouldn't do any good to talk about the bad things – they're over. The good things were getting your letters and hearing from the weans and knowing you and them would be here when I got back – not everybody was so lucky.

You know the Gerries treated us as well as they could – I don't hate them. They were just like us: poor saps sent to fight, not knowing what it was all about. I got quite friendly with some of them, when we were billeted out, just the way they got friendly with some of our people." Before I had thought it out I was telling her about Freda:

"She was just about your age and her man was missing somewhere in Russia. She worked on the farm with us and I used to get going to the local shop with her because I could speak a bit of the lingo – I knew what to ask for for the other prisoners. We were allowed to buy wee things, like Polish fags, when they had any. Anyway, I'm going to be straight with you May; it didn't mean I thought any the less of you, but it was bound to happen…"

I saw the colour washed out of her cheeks by tears… "I was lonely and so was she. I'm sorry May, I couldnae help myself, a couple of times we sneaked away… We'd have been shot if we'd been caught, but it didn't seem to matter. I don't know what happened to her after we were liberated. I hope her man came back safe like I did to you. She was not a bad lass – just lonely."

"Oh John," she was shaking her head and smiling. "I'm glad you've told me about Freda. I know how she felt, her man being away and that. Oh John! I didnae know how to tell you, but now that I know about her, I can tell you.

Something bad happened to me, that I never meant you to know, but it's all right now. I thought you wouldnae understand – now I know you will."

The stub of my fag burnt my fingers and I crushed it in the ashtray – I wanted to do something violent with my hands – I was seeing her through mist, as if the room was filling up with foul yellow smoke.

"What are you on about? Something bad happened to you?"

She then told me about the Polish soldier – riding her in a filthy shed and getting her up the spout. I felt like covering my ears. She was just like a' these other tarts that had written to tell their men that they hadnae been able to wait and were expecting weans tae other men. 'Dear John' letters the lads called them and I had always been so proud that it had never happened to me. May would never do that to me.

She was telling me that he had forced her, and about how she'd had the wean done away wi' – an abortion! I couldnae look at her!

Thant was the end of May and me. I couldnae forgive he. She thought her Pole was the same as me and Freda and I couldnae bring myself to explain the difference.

She kept trying to talk to me about it for a few days and then gave up. I cannae explain why I was the way I was, but I couldnae look at her without feeling bitter water, brash at the back of my throat. I put a pillow between her and I in the bed, knowing that I would have been as well givin' her a hiding – it couldn't have hurt her more. I felt like a bastard for what I was doing but I couldnae help it.

The answer came in the post at the end of that week. The army wanted me back to fight the 'terrorists' in Malaya and I couldn't wait to go. Everything I had said about bringing up the family together and building a good life, meant nothing compared with the need to get away. It wasn't just the thing with May and the Pole but I could have put up with everything else if it hadn't been for that – it was the boredom of doing a job a monkey could have done and working with men who had less intelligence than monkeys and the constant struggle to be a part of the family. They still clammed up when I entered the room; if they had been laughing, they stopped. The progress I had made with some of them was wiped out by the stony barriers the others kept up and I could see by their worried glances that they knew there was something wrong between their mammy and me and I must be to blame.

I went for a few pints before I went home on the Friday night as usual and called them together when I got in, to tell them I was going away again – probably for three years.

I didn't expect them to be put out too much by my news but I didn't want them to hate me. I wanted them to know that I wasn't deserting them – although I was.

I gave them a wee pep talk about looking after each other and helping their mammy. "It's only three years," I said, "and when I get back I'll have managed to save some money and I'll get a better job and a better house in a nicer place than this. This was never meant to be forever."

Vicky and Nancy nodded in agreement but I could see that they were dying to get back to what they had been doing – plucking their eyebrows. Conn and Roddy seemed pleased that I was trusting them to look after the others. May spoke once before poking viciously at the fire – she always took her anger out on the fire.

"What are you going away for?" she asked. "You're no' long back. I thought you were happy to be back in Govan."

"I need a better job. That's all it is," I answered – feeling like a shite.

Billy smiled at me for the first time ever and only Maggie, of all my children, shed a tear and got a row from her big sister for doing it. I would have liked to give her a cuddle. I would have liked to give them all a cuddle. It wasn't the kind of thing we did in the Wallace family.

Once they were all in bed, May cried and argued with me nearly all night. She knew why I was going but it didn't make any difference, I was away before the weans got up in the morning.

*

The three years in Malaya were like a piece out of the jigsaw of someone' else's life. Like the time in Germany, they had nothing to do with the bigger picture of mine.

*

When I came back to wine Alley, I still couldn't find the right place for myself. The family had moved on without my help, but it was a bit better in some ways.

Nancy had joined WRAF and seemed to be enjoying the life, learning to be a nurse. It wouldn't be long before she was telling us she had found a man she wanted to marry. I felt proud of the way she had made her choice about what she wanted to do with her life (Even although I guessed part of it was she fancied herself in uniform – it wasn't important) and just went ahead with it.

I wasn't so happy about Vicky. My plan for curing her crush on the fella from next door – a Catholic and a layabout – hadn't worked. The wedding was all over and they were going to live with us until they got a place of their own. I blamed May for letting her get involved wi' the big clown and she blamed me for the daft letter I had written telling Vicky I would give her a 'big wedding' if only she would wait 'till I came home. I thought if she waited long enough, she would find a decent bloke and he would be ditched.

Well – she hadn't waited, but it had not been exactly the 'big wedding' I had pictured for my oldest daughter. The first drawback was the bridegroom: there was nothing about him I could like and May and the weans were the same. Two family traits: fastidiousness and the inability to suffer fools gladly made us feel more hostile to him than other families might have.

His looks offended the first of these.

We were conceited people about looks and although he had a really good, strong, straight build, the trouble which made his eyes lashless and permanently red, disgusted us rather than made us feel sorry for him. Nobody in the family ever mentioned this but we instinctively knew how each other felt about it. It was the same kind of feeling that made us grue at snotty noses and bad smells – even fat people evoked it. His second and probably worst offence was that he was uneducated and ignorant – not completely his fault because he had missed a lot of schooling because of the illness which had caused the offending eyes – which made us despise him openly.

Poor Vicky tried to improve him constantly.

She bought him Golden eye ointment and even clothes to replace the jersey and trousers, tucked into willies, which was his usual outfit. She even tried to involve him in the word games and quizzes I had taught the weans to play – but it was too embarrassing for all of us and she at last gave up, saying the games were daft anyway and her brothers and sisters were a lot of 'big headed show offs'.

The second drawback for a 'big wedding' was that none of big Terry's family would go, because Vicky was still a protestant.

May told me what she had done when she found out about her taking instruction to join the faith and I was proud of her. I didn't hate Catholics as people but I hated the bastarding religion and what it did to people. I had firsthand experience, believe me. Technically I'm probably one of them – having been forced to take my 'first communion' by my dirty auld sod of a father and his hoor of a wife. I never wanted anyone belonging to me having anything to do with the evil thing.

Nancy and wee Maggie both gave me their versions of the 'big wedding' when I came home: Nancy when I met her at the station, when she came home for a ten days leave, when she'd finished her basic training (She was going in for nursing) and I wanted to walk down Sauchiehall Street with her in her uniform and Maggie when she and I were watching the wean while May was out for the messages on a Saturday morning.

"It was awful," Nancy said. "I felt really sorry for Vicky. She looked beautiful and he kept making stupid jokes that were not the least bit funny." I noticed the trace of an English twang and had a wee laugh to myself – she'd only been there five minutes! What would she sound like after a year or two?

"He wouldn't even have a drink afterwards – and guess where he took her for their first night?"

I already knew, but she was enjoying talking about the horror of it, so I shook my head. "Where?"

"You know that funny wee bowly-legged auntie o' Terry's?" she asked and I notice the English accent had disappeared.

"I thought the whole clan was bowly-legged," I laughed. Born in the saddle and never rode a horse!"

"I think her name's Minnie or something like that," she went on. "Well that's where he took her – tae a room in that wee bachle's house. I felt really sorry for her, lookin' like a film star and being takin' tae a tenement in Chooker Hill for your honeymoon." She blushed when she said honeymoon. "In a way it was really funny. Conn and I kept giggling after they left us to the tramcar – he didn't even get a taxi from the registry office and Vicky paid for the one we took there from Kellas Street. Mind you, we did get a fish tea but I bet Vicky paid for that as well."

"What did you two do after that?" I asked.

She took a wee while to answer and suddenly spotted something really interesting in the tobacconist's window we were passing. "Well," she sighed. "We were really disappointed. You know how you feel when you get brammed up for something good to happen and then it disnae?" She didn't wait for an answer.

"Well, I know he was underage, but I took Conn for a couple of pints in a nice pub at the top of Buchanan Street. He was a bit sick after it, but he was fine."

"That's ma daughter!" I thought, but gave her a quick wee lecture for getting her sixteen-year-old brother drunk and going into a pub without a man to protect her. She said she never worried about needing to be protected.

"Men don't bother me," she said. "I just laugh at them and turn away. I'm used to them making jokes about my red hair and other things. It's only fun."

I suppose I was a coward but I didn't ask what the 'other things' were. For the thousandth time I marvelled at how different from one another my three daughters were.

When I asked Maggie about the wedding, she looked as if she was going to cry. One of the things I had learned about the family was that she was the one that showed her feelings. May was quite cruel to her about it.

"You're like a Christmas card – always greetin'," was one of the jokes she made about her crying over sad stories in the papers or the books she always seemed to have her nose stuck into.

"At first, when Vicky came out of the room in her beautiful powder-blue dress and hat," she began, getting herself into whatever part she was playing. "I felt a lump in my throat. She looked like Lauren Bacall, with her hair shining – I think she put a rinse in it – and her cheeks all flushed. She was the loveliest person I'd ever seen and Nancy was nearly as good. She looked like Rita Hayworth and the colour of the uniform really went with red hair. Conn looked really white and scared but like a grownup man at the same time. It made me feel shaky and shivery inside – like I wanted to laugh, shout and cry – I was really proud that they were my sisters and brother and I was angry too that the rest of us were not going to the wedding.

It was spoilt when HE walked in the door. He looked a lot better than I'd ever seen him, in a new suit that Mammy told us Vicky had bought him. But he was still not good enough for her. She should have somebody like Stewart Granger or Clark Gable, because she was as good as any film star. It was like Beauty and the Beast. I don't think we'd have felt so bad if he'd even looked proud of her and showed that he knew how lucky he was to be marrying her, but he just grabbed her by the arm – you could see it hurt – and said 'Come on, let's get it over with, before the neighbours come out.' A lot of then did come out and threw confetti and shouted things, but Mammy made us stay inside. She wouldn't even let us look out the window."

"Do you think Vicky'll be happy?" she asked me after her description of the wedding.

I just rubbed her hair and said, "She'd better be! Go and put the kettle on for your mammy coming home. I think I'll go for a pint. Tell her I'll no' be long. I didn't like leaving her but I had to go; I couldn't listen to any more about Vicky's wedding.

I blamed May.

She should have made her wait until I came home – then at least it would have been a proper wedding. I knew it would never be a proper marriage. I should have remembered how thrawn she was even as a wee girl.

As soon as May destroyed the rosary and prayer book, Vicky would be determined to defy everyone and marry him as soon as possible. My idea had been to talk her into waiting with the promise of a 'big white wedding' so that she would see that she had nothing in common with him – I wasn't sure if he could even read – and find somebody of her own class and hopefully not a bloody catholic.

May blamed me.

"If you hadnae decided to swan off and leave everything to me, it would never have happened," she said when I was saying for the hundredth time that she should never have allowed her to give him the time of day, far less let them winch in our lobby every night (Nancy had told me about that too).

Still, it was done. I just hoped she wouldn't have weans to him – his mother had had thirteen – before she saw sense.

*

The next thing was Nancy writing to tell us she was bringing a fella to meet us on her next leave. I would soon be losing another daughter, I supposed. At least this one wasn't a catholic and he was in the RAF, so he must be reasonably smart. In the army we had always sneered at them 'Brylcreem Boys' but it was only a laugh. We knew that it took as much guts to do what they did as it did for us to do what we did. It was all part of the same thing – fighting for your country – although I was never too sure about that.

I had been in the army, first time because I had to be and second time to get away from a life that was not for me and try to make a better life for my family. The king and country thing had always been a bit suspect to me. I loved Scotland – William Wallace, Robert Burns and all that but what I had seen and what I had read, had convinced me that the only real losers in war were the poor working class mugs like me, that were sent off to be cannon fodder.

Vera Lynn singing that line from 'The White Cliffs of Dover' "…and Johnny will go to sleep in his own little room again.," always gave me the boak.

I'd never had 'my own little room', nor had any of the other weans I was brought up with, or my own weans – even though we were now better off than we had ever been as regards housing. I could see that it was all just part of the big con played on us by our 'betters' from the day we were born.

Nancy's wedding was a big affair by the standards of Wine Alley at that time, but it was not good enough. I knew she deserved better – any young girl does on her wedding day – but there just wasn't the money around. Her dress was hired and her veil borrowed from my cousin; I managed to get some material from the docks for Vicky and Maggie's dresses and we got Conn and Roddy suits on tick, but they were the best looking wedding party ever, despite the clown I had paid to take photos making an arse of them – he was drunk as a monkey and I gave him a sore face for it.

We held the reception in the house and everything went well until my cousin, Jimmy Osbourne, gate crashed. I really like the boy. His mother, my Auntie Kate, had always been really good to me when I'd been forced to live with the hoor my dad had married, letting me have a bath at her house and making sure I got fed. But he really blotted his copybook that night.

Everybody was up dancing to the records Conn was playing on the radiogram I had bought and I was just sitting on my chair, laughing and enjoying a glass of the whisky I had managed to get 'under the counter', when I noticed what he was up to.

He had hold of wee Maggie and he was whirling her around like a madman. Her blouse was way up around her neck, showing off her bare skin and her skirt was pulled up, showing her knickers.

I made one breenge at him and grabbed him round the neck, pulling Maggie away from him at the same time. All I could hear was women screaming above my own voice saying: "She's only thirteen ya bastard. I'm gonna kill you."

A couple of the men grabbed hold of me, or I might have killed the poor sod. Something about seeing the wee lassies exposed like that had detonated a mad rage in my brain. I didn't stop to think that he meant no harm. It felt as though I was watching her being violated. He let her go, both of them looking totally mystified and she ran out the door – the tears tripping her – and a couple of the women took him by the arms and led him out. He was shaking his head like someone who wants to be forgiven but doesn't know what for.

"I'm sorry John," he muttered as he passed me.

"You will be, the next time I see you," I shouted, trying to get free of the hands that held me.

Later, when the excitement had died down and everybody was away, I sat smoking by what was left of the fire. I felt embarrassed at making a clown of myself. Jimmy was no pervert. It had been a stupid mistake – I could see that. Yet the rage still boiled within me when the picture of him pulling and hauling at her thin, wee body kept pushing its way into my mind. I'd never felt like this before about any of my weans, I once did fly at a waiter that had looked the wrong way at May – but that had been jealousy that another man should be thinking thoughts about my wife that only I was meant to think.

I couldna be jealous of my own daughter? No I saw how innocent she was, actually enjoying the attentions of a man – and that's what had made me mad. It wasn't jealousy. That would be stupid.

Jimmie came a couple of days later to sort things out between us – we'd always been great pals. He brought his girlfriend, a nice plump, wee thing, and nearly died of shame when wee Maggie came in from school in her school uniform, looking about seven instead of thirteen.

"You were quite right, John," he said. "I might have hurt the wee lass, swinging her around like that but I never meant her any harm. It was the drink."

After that I paid more attention to my youngest daughter. She had always made more of an attempt to accept me, ever since that first day back, but I had got taken up with other things and forgot she was there. Now she became my main occupation when I was in the house. I even thought of her sometimes when I was at work or in the pub.

Maybe it was because the rest of them were getting on with their own lives: Vicky and Nancy with their married lives; Conn with his talent shows and Roddy with his engineering apprenticeship – his employers thought the world of him and he was going out with the foreman's daughter.

Billy still lived in his self-contained life that I was never allowed into and wee Jay was just a baby yet, so all I had really was Maggie.

She was the oddest looking wee thing – too wee for her age – with thick straight hair which hadn't made up its mind what colour to be and eyes that took up her whole face and which were usually glued to a book.

I watched her sitting at the living room table every night, doing her homework, borrowing my fountain pen for her 'ink exercises', biting her lip and stopping to cough a lot. I watched her playing secret games with Billy that nobody else was allowed into (she told me later that they made up codes for each other to decipher). I watched her especially when she would curl up into a ball on the couch, or the armchair opposite me and, oblivious of showing off her ragged school knickers, read for hours, her face sliding from one emotion to the other as she read.

The house could have fallen down or gone on fire and she would have stayed in her book world. Sometimes I asked what she was reading – she read everything from Jane Austen to the Woman's Weekly romances – but she could only spare me a second or two to answer my questions before she disappeared back into the pages.

It drove May mad, her reading.

"She's a lazy wee bitch," she said. "She's always reading or out wi' her pals. I've got to tell her if I want the table set or the dishes done."

I never argued – it would just make things worse.

"Have you had her to the doctor yet, with that cough?" I asked.

"He says there's nothing wrong with her, just her age," she answered, going red at even the hint that sex might have anything to do with the girl's illness. I'd never even heard her say the word 'period' in all the years we'd been married. She called her monthly cycle 'that time' or 'a visitor', anything to avoid discussing anything physical. She'd been brought up in the belief that all that sort of thing was dirty and the punishment women had to suffer for being women.

"He says she might just be trying to get off school. He says lasses of that age are always trying to get off."

"Take her back to see him and if he still says that, tell him you want to see another doctor," I told her, listening to the hacking cough that was coming from the girl's room.

*

I sometimes blamed May for listening too long to that fool of a doctor, but I knew that she wasn't really to blame. I remembered my sister Maggie, the symptoms were the same. I should have known she had consumption – as we called it then – and was glad in a way when she got an X-ray that confirmed it.

It was that and what happened to Vicky that made me decide that we had to get out of the Wine Alley and find a better place for the rest of the weans to grow up.

I really thought they would all be happy when I told them we were getting a brand new five-apartment house (wi' a back and front door) as part of the bribery Rolls Royce was using to lure workers to their big aircraft factory in the new town of East Kilbride.

"We'll be miles away from everything," Roddy said, but he came round when I said he could get a good job there. Conn was trying to get into a singing career in London, so he didn't count and Nancy and Vicky had their own lives.

I was doing it for Maggie. She was going into a sanatorium – maybe she wouldn't come out – but when she did I wanted her to have a clean, decent place to live. Billy didn't say whether he wanted to go or not, but he couldn't have been happy to leave his pals and wee Jay was too young to care.

May hated the thought of flitting (in among a lot of snobs) as she put it, but the thought of not having to take her turn of the stairs or fight for drying green swayed her.

Wine Alley was meant to be a new beginning for us as a family – for some it had been. Yet I knew there must be something better. At least May and I could try to build something for what was left of the family. Maybe I could forget the one bad thing she had done and live as a married couple again.

On a Saturday morning, Rangers were playing Aberdeen so Roddy was not happy. We squeezed into two vans, borrowed from a pal of mine, and left the dirty grey harl and the strange experience of Wine Alley days behind us forever.

MORE MAGGIE

The Register teacher – Mrs Halliday – called the six of us out individually and gave us a sealed brown envelope – to be taken home unopened.

"Better keep away from that lot" Billy MacDonald, the unfunny class clown said as we changed classes. "They must have the dreaded lurgies or something". I kicked him really hard on this ankle bone as he sidled past, and that shut him up.

"Come on into the toilets," I said to Isa. "I want to see what's in this." It was a note from the Head – we should have guessed – listing 'the basic dress requirements for school' and asking our Mammys to "make every effort to see that your child is properly dressed". He had announced to the whole school assembly that morning that a few pupils were 'letting the side down by not making an effort to wear the school uniform – a red or grey shirt blouse, navy gym slip or grey trousers (boys) and a red and black striped tie.

"Your school is somewhere to be proud of and wearing the uniform shows others that you go to a school with such a wonderful academic and sporting record of achievement. "He went on in this vein for about ten minutes (obviously forgetting the proportion of pupils who were on probation, or had been transferred to approved schools, for one reason or another) and his towering figure, in its black beetle-wing gown seemed to look down on us from a mountain of superiority and he had the effect on me, if on no one else, of convincing me that I had to wear this uniform to single me out in the eyes of an envious world – well Govan anyway – as a pupil of this wonderful school.

I had been at the High school for a week by then and was one of only six of the class who did not have some semblance of school uniform. No matter that May had bought me new shoes and a grey and red striped jumper to go with one of Vicky's cut down skirts – I had to have the uniform.

"Is your register teach going to pay for this uniform? "May asked, throwing down the cutlery for me to set the table.

"No, but I'm the only one in my year that hasn't got it," I lied. "And we're the top section. They'll probably put me down to a lower class if I don't get it "Such was the weight of the guilt I put on her, she got a, provi cheque that very night, to share between Billy and I (She hoped if she got him new clothes he might go to school instead of hiding in the raid shelters, or going to the park).

I got a tie and a new gymslip, but there wasn't enough for a blouse or gym kit, so she dyed one of Nancy's old blouses red and I had to share gym trunks with Roddy: Sometimes we had to pass them between us in the corridor like the baton in a relay race, if we were having PE on the same day. I pretended he was giving them to me to take home for him, or the other way around – I knew nobody believed me, but they7 did not say anything.

The girls in the 'big school' didn't ridicule me they way they had once done in the Primary. I was top in almost every subject, I was funny and nice looking in an "orpan Annie" kind of way and IU had my own little clique of friends. There were six of us: Katie, Isa and myself plus June McShane, Lizzie McLean and Pearl Watson. There was Margaret Park as well, but she was off school a lot, so missed out on a lot of our goings on. Our main interest was boys and some of the teachers, male and female.

There was one teacher we drove to a nervous breakdown. I can still see his wild eyes as he pulled at his thin gingery hair and yelled at us sending spit flying in all directions. This was what we wanted; what we had been working towards. No matter how hard he tried to interest us in his subject – French – we baited, ignored or ridiculed him depending on our mood. We were like the seagulls I once watched on a beach, attacking one of their own who was too weak to fly away or fight back.

His name was Mr Burnett and our form teacher, probably trying to get us on his side, told us he was the most brilliant teacher in the school and we were lucky to have him. This made us worse:

"If he's such a brilliant teacher," one of the boys said, as we waited to inflict our almost daily torture on him, "why can't he control his classes?" We were the top academic class, taking Latin as well as French. There were thirty-four of us. The kind of pupils that teachers and parents imagine, would never cheek a teacher or misbehave in any way. But we had brought bad behaviour into the arena of psychological warfare and Mr Burnett, for no reason we could have explained was our victim. Shouting, pleading, raving, giving punishment exercises, belting, sending to the Head, and even rushing from the room and staying away for the rest of the period with a mouse; snakes mesmerising mongooses; boys pulling the wings off flies. It started as a bit of fun when he first hit himself on the leg when he was trying to belt Alan Trotter, the best looking, nicest boy in the class and got darker and more savage every time we entered his room and saw the hunted look in his eyes and his thin hands playing with a piece of chalk, lie Captain Queeg in the Caine Mutiny playing with his beads.

As soon as we sat down in the class, the girls would start playing consequences – apart from a few decent souls who felt sorry for him and tried to look interested in his attempts to teach a lesson – a game which meant passing pieces of paper around and giggling or screeching at what was written there. The boys would draw on one another's shirts, whistle, fart in tune and throw paper aeroplanes – one someone set fire to the wastepaper basket, and another time they stuck his board duster to the ceiling so that he could not remove the selection of penises and fannies that a previous class had drawn on every section of the roller board.

I was the leader among the girls and he kept me behind one day after the period, to appeal to my better nature: "You could help me to get the others to pay attention," he said, "You're the best in the class at French, but you are all falling behind, because of the silly behaviour that goes on. A clever girl like you must now that. I don't want always to be giving punishments. I want to get on with my top class." I stared at him, saying nothing, until he lifted the lid of his desk and hid his face, pretending to be looking for something. I was shocked at the thoughts of destruction that came into my head as I watched the tears gathering in the corner of his eyes. "Why do you behave so badly in *my* class?" he whined. "There's nothing but good reports from your other teachers. Tell me what is wrong and I will try to put it right." The power he was handing to me was making me mad. I wanted to laugh and dance around him like people did in the middle-ages when they watched witches being burnt at the stake, but I managed to control myself and think how I could use his 'little chat' against him and to enhance my position as leader over the girls.

Some people may think what we did next day was funny – I did for a while – bit it pushed him out of teaching and into a mental ward:

His was the first period after the morning interval, so we had time to prepare the 'joke'. He even tried to join in, with a scared little laugh when the first few of us walked into the room. We had spent part of the interval putting our shirts and ties on backwards and walked backwards into the room.

"This is not funny!" he yelled as we sat down – apart from the three 'good' girls – with our back to him, so that he was looking at the backs of heads, above the fronts of shirts and ties. We got out our paper and pencils and started our games of consequences.

"Bastards!" He didn't shout but there was enough venom in that one word to make even my hackles stand on end. He walked out of the door stumbling over his own feet, for our amusement. Ten minutes passed before he returned, bringing the Headmaster, to be faced with us all, sitting facing the front and dressed normally. That was it. That was the end of him. He just shook his head and shuffled out of the room. We never saw him again, but we heard that he would be on sick-leave for a long time.

*

Mr Andy Mason was a different kind of teacher from Mr Burnett. Some people would call him a 'natural'. He taught English and his first post began as Isa, Katie, June and Liz and I entered our third year at High school. The boys didn't care for him as he was much harder on them than he was on the girls. The girls adored him. To be adored by adolescent girls is a dangerous position for any man to be in, but poor Andy did not see the danger, until the Head sent for him, to explain himself to June McShane's dad.

He was holding her 'School Friends Diary' in his hand. The pupils got to know about it through the chain of communication that linked the Head's secretary to her sister the head cleaner, to her man and through their overheard conversation, to their daughter who started the spread throughout the school, but, worse still for poor Andy – somebody phoned the papers.

It had started as a game. All of us who were in love with Andy wrote things in our diary about him and passed our fantasies around the group the next day. The entries were ridiculous (as any sane person could see) but Mr McShane, stirred up by his wife, was convinced that his daughter had been the victim of the lurid sexual practices she had credited her teacher with performing.

Poor Andy. What could he say against the written evidence in the diary of a thirteen-year-old girl. Whatever he said, no-one believed him. The Head told him he had ruined a promising career and to go home and wait for a letter from the Education Authority. His wife of six months moved back in with her mother and took the dog with her.

The newspapers had a field day:

"PERVERT TEACHER FOUND OUT BY GIRL'S FURIOUS FARTHER"

Was one of the less judgemental headlines, accompanied by extracts from the diary. Thank God nobody had found mine. It was much worse.

JUNE'S DAIRY

<u>Mon. May 1st</u>: Saw Mr Mason our new English teacher for the first time to-day. He is a doll. His name is Andy. He told us. I felt really embarrassed during the lesson. He couldn't take his eyes off me. I'm going to dream about him tonight.

<u>Wed. May 3rd</u>: It's obvious Andy wants me. He squeezed by arm when he leaned over my desk and 'accidently' rubbed himself against me when I was out at the bookshelf. I want him to touch every bit of me with his strong brown hands.

<u>Mon. May 15th</u>: Any pulled me into the bookstore to-day and shoved his hands inside my blouse. He played around with me

until I nearly screamed out. I wanted him to put the hairy monster into me but he says I'll have to wait. I dream of him doing it to me every night.

She passed the diary around as we sat in our secret place at the back of the gym hall and we all pretended to be shocked, but we did not have to pretend when we read Liz's entry for the same period.

LIZ'S DIARY

<u>Mon 1st May:</u> At last something good has happened in this fucking school. Our new English teacher has arrived and he keeps making come to bed eyes at me. My knickers get wet just listening to his voice. His name is Mr Mason, Andy to me, and he only need to ask and I'll let him ride me to death.

<u>Wed 3rd May:</u> Andy slid his hand up my back when he was marking my jotter, and loosened my bra. I nearly shit myself in case anybody saw him, but he just gave me a big wink and said in front of the whole class that I had to stay behind at the interval and discuss my work. He tore the knickers off me as soon as the door shut behind the rest of the class. What he did next was wicked, but I didn't want to stop him.

<u>Mon 15th May:</u> He put IT in my hand to-day and I nearly fainted. It's enormous. I wanted to feel it inside me, but he told me he wanted to wait until we could meet away from the school. I kissed it for him instead and he swore like a madman. I don't know what might have happened if the bell hadn't gone.

We played the game all that term: each writing in her diary the filthy exploits of the perfectly innocent Mr Mason, who was a happily married man, until he fell a victim to our adolescent sex-madness.

By mid-June, when Mr McShane found the diary, the pages described the actions of a monster of depravity and the bookstore had become the venue for every sexual fantasy fourteen-year-old girls could dream up, with Andy as the seducer and we four as the seduced. Luckily only one diary was found and June's imagination was the least lurid of the four of us, but it was enough for the parents of Govan to be sharpening their shears for a castration.

When the women in the close found out that me and my 'two wee pals' (Isa and Katie) had the monster as a teacher, they looked at us with a new respect. They had always called me 'a snooty wee bitch' before; now they looked at me in the same way as most people look at the photos of murder victims in the papers – with a thin veil of sympathy hiding the lust of detail, the more disgusting and depraved the better.

"It's enough to turn a young lassie against men for life," Mrs Ranachan announced to the other members of the Number 16 coven as we three sat hanging out of my bedroom window just above the close. She knew we were there and was probably hinting for some information from us. To my horror Isa gave it to her:

"He was a really good teacher", she said, "He always seemed so nice" she even managed a little throat – catching sob.

"Aye, it's always the nice yins!" came from down below like the ghost of Hamlet's father.

"Shut up." I dug Isa in the ribs. "You would think it was all true to hear you. It was only a game".

"I don't know what Johnnie Wallace is thing of," was said in a Ranachan whisper that I was meant to hear. "Letting his lass still go to that school. In the old days he would've cut the cock off the dirty pig". There followed shrieks of dirty laughter at the very thought of such a thing. I wondered if that was what they would like to see done to their own men.

It was Mammy who first brought up the subject with me. I was standing in the kitchenette, waiting for her to fill up the dinner plates, for me to take through to the living room, when she said, her face scarlet, "I hope you haven't been havin' anything to do with this dirty nonsense that's been going on at the school – have you?"

"No, of course not." I grabbed a plate and ran, spilling gravy everywhere. That was bad enough – having my mother even hint that she knew about 'dirty things', but it was not nearly as bad as Daddy, taking me out for a walk to find out if there was anything he should know about that 'evil bloke'.

"You're a nice looking lassie," he said to me, "but you are only a wee lassie, too young for any man to be thinking of that kind of thing with you – far less a teacher."

While he was talking – he was holding me by the hand – I suddenly saw, in my mind, Andy Mason's serious face as he had tried to explain Hamlet to us.

"The lassie is in my class right enough," I said. "But she says she was only making it all up – about Mr Mason – it's just that her Dad won't believe her."

"He's quite right. Why would a young lassie make up things like that? There must be something in it. You're sure he never tried anything with you? According to the papers he used to get her on her own in the book store. Were you ever in there with him? You can tell me. I'll keep it between us." He quizzed, squeezing my hand. I wished I could find the nerve to tell him about the game we had been playing, but I couldn't bear to have him think badly of me. I wanted praise from him not condemnation, although goodness knows I deserved it.

What if he found my diary? He wouldn't. I had slid it behind the gas fire in my room. It was never used. The tap was so rusted it would not turn. I was safe.

MY DIARY

<u>Tues May 2nd</u>: To-day I met the man of my dreams. He looks like a poet, with lovely shiny dark hair and really moody eyes. His name is Andy Mason and I know from the way he looks at me that he is as attracted to me as I am to him.

<u>Wed May 10th</u>: Andy touched my hand to-day, as he was marking my jotter. I can still feel it tingling. I dreamt he was touching me all over. I stroked myself, pretending it was him and I early shouted out loud, it made me feel so good.

<u>Wed May 17th</u>: To-day, a man touched me there for the first time. It was Andy. Who else would I let touch me. He said he wants to go the whole way with me and he's going to take me on a date. I can't wait.

<u>Sat May 20th</u>: I'm a woman at last. Andy did it to me in the bluebell woods. He said I was wonderful and he wants to do it to me again and again. I thought a man's thing would be dirty and ugly but his is beautiful, but awful big.

<u>Mon May 22nd</u>: This will be the last I'll write for a while. I'll have to hide my diary. It's all June McShane's fault. She's been writing lies about Andy in her diary and her Dad found it. He's showed it to the Head and Andy's in terrible trouble. It'll be alright when she tells them she made it all up.

The newspaper story read:

"A young male teacher 'a married man', has been charged in connection with allegations of interfering with a girl pupil, made by the girl's father, whom we are not allowed to name in order to protect the girl's identity. He did say to our reporter "Any teacher who takes advantage of his position of trust to try to have sex with a pupil should be severely punished. Jail is too good for such a monster.

*

It was Isa who first said, "We'll have to tell somebody about the game." The girls in 3A had been so upset when they read the story about their hero – who was really a monster – that some of them had to be sent home; others spent the rest of the day in the medical room, crying their eyes out. Our little clique had agreed to meet up in my house, after school and we had had to walk through a sighing and patting from the close women, who hadn't been so close to a good scandal, since the woman up the street had shoved her man out of the third storey window: "Keep yer chin up", "A know whit a would like tae dae tae him", "Think yourself lucky", and "Bloody monster" were some of the words of the chorus as we hurried in the close, keeping our heads down, in shame.

"Who can we tell?" Katie said, pushing her glasses up her nose. "My mammy would kill me. She thinks I don't know anything. If she knew what I had written; she would kill me even though it's not true."

"What if we do tell and nobody believes us?" Liz said and I nodded thinking what Daddy had said. Would anybody believe that young girls like us could make up such filthy things. What if we made it worse for him?

"How can it be any worse?" Isa said. "He'll lose his job definitely; his wife will probably leave him and he might even go to jail – What can be worse than that for somebody who was always really nice to us. I'm going to tell somebody. I just don't know who yet."

We finally decided on telling Miss Halliday – our form teacher, hoping that she could save Andy without bringing our parents into it.

The five of us sat in front of her desk and I spoke up for all of us. I told her about the game, how we had thought it was just a bit of fun and nobody would ever know about it but us. I told her what a good teacher Andy was. I told her that he had never touched any of us and certainly hadn't done any of the things we had written in our diaries. June had been telling the truth when she told her father it was all made up. For proof we all laid our Schoolfriend Diaries on the desk in front of her.

Her moustache stood on end like angry cat's fur as she read one diary after the other, throwing them at the owners as she finished.

"Disgusting little tarts!" she said finally, spraying us with spit.

We were all in tears by the end, except Isa who kept her sharp little nose in the air as if to say: "OK, we know we're disgusting – what now?"

"Are you going to tell our mums and dads? Please don't. We're really sorry."

Liz snivelled and Pearl and Katie joined in, "Please Miss we're really sorry."

"I'll have to see what the Head says." She stood up, gathering the diaries as if she didn't really want to dirty her hands on them. "Get to your classes now. You'll be sent for."

It was well into the afternoon when the Head's secretary came and collected us from our classes. The Head's room was pretty crowded when I arrived. My pals were already there but I hardly noticed them. The Head was seated at his desk, like a judge without a wig and behind him stood the biggest, reddest faced polis I had ever seen, who was looking at us as if his eyes would leave his head and attack us any minute. On the right of the desk, seated, was Andy Mason, avoiding looking at us and holding the hand of a pale, pasty young woman who was seated beside him – his wife – I thought; on the left was Miss Halliday, holding the diaries. Even Isa was greeting by the time we left that room – minus our diaries and our self esteem. Firstly the Head had totally humiliated us by comparing our behaviour to that of criminals and pornographers and shuddered to think what our parents would think; then we were made to apologise to Andy and his wife, both of whom found it impossible to look at us; then Miss Halliday made each of us in turn tear up our diaries and put them in the Head's wastepaper basket. Finally, the huge navy-clad figure stepped forward and made us line up in front of him.

"I am empowered," he began, eyes scanning our souls, "to administer a caution to you on the condition that you Headmaster vouches for your good behaviour in the future. For the time being your criminal malicious behaviour will remain within these four walls, but if any of you as much as mention Mr Mason's name in the future, your parents will be informed and criminal proceedings instituted.

I do not know how legal the whole business was, but a tiny column in the next day's paper said that all charges against the 'local teacher' had been dropped as it had been discovered that he was the victim of malicious gossip by pupils.

We didn't see him again; he got a transfer to Inverness and June McShane dropped out of our little gang so we never heard what her father thought of the whole thing.

Soon there were more interesting things happening in Wine Alley.

*

I always loved the long summer nights in Wine Alley. As soon as the dinner was by in all the houses, weans appeared out of the closes like bees leaving their hive in search of pollen, while the mammys stayed in, just like the queen bee, but unlike her, emerging, usually around eight o'clock to take up their positions at the closemouth, or on really good nights to join in the games of skipping ropes and rounders.

Once the games were over, the women talked, until sometimes well after midnight. Usually the weans were chased off to bed around nine or ten, but Flora Hood and I used to hide out of the way in a corner – missing the curfew and listening to things we weren't meant to hear.

It was during one of those sessions we hear about the rape:

Maisie Ranachan started it. We knew by the sound of her voice that she was speaking up to where Ma Wilson was hingin' oot at her window (She never sat in the close, but joined in, like some modern Madame Defarge, from her 'gallery').

"Have ye ever hear the likes o' that lassie Cleary?" she began, "Accusing four lads anyway, eh?"

"Nae better than her mither or any o' that family," wee Mrs Bredin, put in. "Nane o' them know who their faithers are."

"Aye, they're aw the same – cannae keep their legs shut – dirty hoors." The voice from above, made me squeeze Flora's hand that tight that she gave a wee squeal of pain, but nobody noticed, they were too busy agreeing and joining in the devouring of 'that lassie Cleary's ' character.

I got a sudden picture of her in my mind – a skinny, sick-looking gypsy of a girl, with eyes that always looked as if she had been crying, broken teeth and spectacular long wavy black hair, like flowing tar – she was about three years older than me, which would make her sixteen. I had never seen her out with a lad. In fact the lads laughed at her scruffy clothes and shouted names after her. What had they done to her that was making the closemouth witches so excited and vicious? I badly needed to know.

"Four o' the lads have been charged, you know."

I couldn't believe it – it was Mammy's voice. She usually let the others do the talking. I alays felt she was still scared of them. She went on.

"They must have done something bad to be charged. I always thought she was a right quiet lassie – maybe a wee bit backward, but a harmless kind o'cratur. She didnae deserve to be raped – nobody does."

"Listen tae it!" Maisie Ranachan sneered. "Rape! None o' that family ever had to be raped. They serve it up as soon as they're able. I bet they lads werenae the first and they'll no be the last. They Clearys just cannae get enough o' it. You don't know what you're talking about."

"They're saying they did terrible things to her." Mrs Murray sounded as if she was apologising for speaking. "I don't think there was any need for that" A cackle sounded from above. "They wouldnae do that to a decent lassie. She asked for it – and who's gonnae believe a puckin' liar like her?" (She always said 'puckin' when she mean the 'F' word. Daddy told us it was because RCs weren't supposed to swear).

"What did they do?"

Mammy again, I was that glad she had asked. I was peeing myself with excitement. There was quite a long silence, as if everyone was waiting for someone else to reveal what they knew. It was a man's voice which broke the silence – one of the Curry lads from the next close. He had been sitting winching Sadie Ranachan, behind Maisie's back. His voice was wet and excited when he spoke:

"They shaved her cunt and cut off most o' her hair," he said. "She's in the Southern General. A heard she's gone right aff her heid. So a did."

"Less o'that talk," Maise checked. "A thought a told you to get inside Sadie Ranachan. De ye want tae feel ma toe in yer arse?" and turning to the boy Curry who had jumped about three feet away from Sadie: "You! Get away back to yer ain close. Waht dae ye want tae be sitting wi' a'the weemin fur? Ye big Jessie, ye."

"Wheesht, let him tell us what he's heard. Talk up son," the voice from the gallery again.

"It's no very nice," he began

"Sadie, get inside now," Maisie yelled and Sadie flounced away, nearly shaking her head off. We thought we were safe, until she saw us and yelled out,

"What about they two? They're a lot younger than me and they're listening."

Mammy turned and saw us. She slapped me on the legs and shoved me upstairs in front of her at the same time saying to Flora, "You better get home to your mother, lady. She'll be wondering where you are."

So we never heard Tim's story, but we did hear what the gossips said about poor Nora Cleary and we got more horrible pleasure out of talking about it than we got from reading 'Forever Amber' that Flora had borrowed out of her big sister's room.

*

It seemed that Norah had been walking across the spare ground that lay between the railway goods yard and the Wine Alley. It was a shortcut most of us took all the time, but not at night and on our own, but it had been a clear summer's night and she must have thought it was quite safe.

Some fellas – stories varied, from four to twenty-four – were kicking a ball into the goal posts somebody had painted on the wall of one of the old shelters. They were bored and when Norah appeared, walking like a cat that has had too many kickings, something got into them. It started when the boy with the ball kicked it directly at Norah, scoring a direct hit on the side of her head, which nearly knocked her off her feet. She stood for a minute, dazed and frightened, smiling with her broken mouth to show that she wasn't angry at being hit, but this seemed to make them mad:

"Give us our ball back, ya tinkie bitch," the lad who had kicked the ball yelled, and before they knew what they were doing they were around her in a circle – kind of dancing around, aiming punches at her, but not actually touching her, the way some animals do before they kill their prey. Maybe nothing would have happened if one of them hadn't suddenly pounced forward and pulled her skirt up, showing her poor skinny white legs and black knickers. For a minute, the others were shocked into shame at her cry:

*

"Oh dinnae dae that!" but only for a minute: one ran at her and spun her round by the hair, laughing at her screams; another put his hand up her skirt and pulled at the leg of her knickers and his pal pulled open the lad's shirt she was wearing tearing apart the safety-pins which covered her modesty.

"Oh naw, dinnae, Oh please, let me be," she sobbed, turning them into animals, instead of the lads out for some mischief.

Stories about what happened after that were wild and wonderful: it was said at the closemouths, with hushed relish that they had not only raped her over and over again and in every way possible, but that they had shaved her pubic hair and stuck rubbish 'up her hole'.

It was true that she was nearly dead when she was found by a man going to work on nightshift, and her clothes were lying in tatters, where she had tried to use them to cover herself. He was a decent man and he never gave out any information, apart from what he gave to the police and in court later, but he moved with his young family, out of the Wine Alley, before the case came to court.

For a while the street was deserted after eight o'clock at night, apart from the closemouth chorus. Weans were sent up the stair and there were no street games, just a feeling of gloating, digust or fear – depending on who you were.

Things went back to normal, until the trial came up. Nora had named four lads, although she said there had been others she didn't know. There was a kind of smug feeling among the women that none of the rapists came from Kellas Street, but Conn and

Roddy told Nancy (Billy and I were listening) that a couple of lads were thanking God that "the tink didnae know their names".

The trial was all that was talked about: one lad, gret and said the rest had made him 'do her'; another said, she had been asking for it; the other two had the grace to hang their heads and admit that they had done it. All four got six years in jail.

Nora got a life of being ridiculed in the street; people moving away from her on buses and giving into any drunk that would take her into the back close and show her that somebody wanted her, even if they usually beat her up afterwards. Her time was served, when her body was found on the banks of the Clyde, five years after the rape. Nobody seemed interested in finding out how she had died.

"It's a bad day when fellas cannae get their candy, without bein' locked up," was Maisie Ranachan's comment on the sentences.

"A decent lassie wouldnae have been walkin, there herself at night" was the opinion of some of the others. Even at my young age and given how much I had been excited by the whole affair since I'd hear about it that night, hiding in the close, I knew that they were wrong, even more so because they were women. I wondered if they would have felt the same if it had been one of their own daughters. I knew they wouldn't. They relished rape, just as much – we discovered – as they relished murder.

*

It was on another summer night that we saw the blackest side of our home town.

It was Friday night and Mammy had taken us to the first house of the pictures as a treat, to see a Western, that everyone was talking about. We had turned up Neptune Street to go to the chip shop, to round off our night. I loved those nights when she took us out. She was a different person – like a young girl, laughing with us and making us take each other's arms, and buying toffee and ices in the interval. We were quite well off at the time.

A skinny red-haired man ran past us as we turned into Neptune Street. A drop of blood from his torn – open face splattered on the shoulder of Mammy's best coat, and she shepherded us up the nearest closemouth as we saw another three men racing after him. They were shouting something involving 'orange' and 'bastard' and I thought for a minute she was going to step out and check them for 'swearing in front of the weans', which we had seen her do before, but instead she pulled us through to the back close, managing to hold the three of us – Billy, Wee Jay and me – at once.

"We can cut across the backs," she said. "We don't want caught up in any fighting – nothing but a lot of mad men, that's what they are."

But it didn't work out like that: when we came out of the back close we were looking at the backs of a ring of bodies – I had a sudden memory of my fight at Ibrox school, but these were not children in a playground fight. They were men and women out for blood.

Mammy couldn't hold us for long – this was better than any picture – Billy and I rushed to get into the ring, but she lifted Wee Jay to stop him following.

"You couldn't call it a fight," Billy said later to me when we were discussing it. "It must have been at least twelve against one. It was the man that ran past us they were kicking – maybe Mammy'll be called as a witness, or something – his blood's on her coat."

It wasn't so much the sight and smell of the blood and god knows what else that made me turn my insides out when we finally were dragged and pushed up the road by Mammy: It was the sound!

The lad on the ground wasn't exactly screaming – it was more of a howl and he was shouting for his Mammy:

"Oh, Mammy, Mammy help me! Oh God help me, Oh Maaammmy and then that awful sobbing howl, worse than any banshee in a nightmare – as they kicked, punched, stamped, dragged and kicked again. And while they wee doing it they were laughing and cursing: "The orange fuckin' scabby bastard!"

We couldn't stop talking about it.

When we finally reached Number 16, Mammy had rushed us past the women at the close. I thought she would want to tell them about it, but since Daddy had come back she 'kept herself to herself'

"What the hell's up?" he asked as she rushed into the living-room, throwing off her coat and pushing us before her at the same time.

"Get to bed you two," she said to us. "Take the wean with you. I'll bring you your supper."

"But it's Friday!" Billy and I whined at the same time. We always got staying up late at the weekends and we were desperate to hear what Daddy would have to say about the fight – maybe he would know some of the men; he knew everybody in Govan.

"What have they done?" he asked lowering his brows at us like an angry terrier.

"Nothing," she flopped down on the nearest chair. "We've just seen a fella being murdered. Oh my God John! It was awful; they kicked him to death."

"Right, you two go and get your Mammy a cup of tea – hand her coat, while you're at it." She grabbed the coat and shoved it behind her on the chair.

"No it'll need tae be flung away; it's got his blood on it – oh my God I was that close to him." She started to sob and wee Jay and I joined in.

"Wheesht," he said softly. "That'll no help. You're just upsetting yourself and the weans. Tell me what happened – you two, get that tea, take the wee fella with you. Give him a biscuit."

While we were making the tea we could hear her voice. We knew it was her, but it sounded more like a wee girl crying as if her heart was broken and he was shushing her, as he did when any of us weans hurt ourselves.

I wanted to carry the two cups of tea through, but I gave in and let Billy carry one and wee Jay followed carrying a plate of biscuits, which was nearly empty by the time he put it on the table between them. Daddy was sitting beside her, trying to get her to drink a glass of sherry and she was looking at him as if she knew that he would make the bogey man go away.

They let us stay up late – as long as we were quiet – and somehow we didn't feel like talking anymore. I got my 'Schoolfriend' out and curled up on a corner of the settee to read it and Billy began drawing in his notebook, with his tongue nearly touching the page. Wee Jay fell asleep on Mammy's knee.

After we were in bed, I heard the front door shut and Mammy came though and put the wean in beside me.

"Your Daddy's gone out for a wee while to see what he can find out". She said, "He says you've no tae talk to anybody about it. If they ask you say you didnae see anything – right?"

"But, what if…?" I interrupted – seeing my role as chief witness disappear.

"No ifs. You've no tae talk about it, your Daddy says. He knows what these people are like. Just let on we saw nothing; Right?"

*

It was in the papers the next day:

"Jimmy Devine, a nineteen-year-old man, was killed in a gangfight, in the back court of Neptune Street last night. It is thought that the fight was between Protestants and Catholics. Two men have been arrested, but not yet named. It is believed that Mr Devine's wife is expecting her first baby."

Billy and I were dying to talk about it – we'd been witnesses to a murder – but a look from either of our parents shut us up.

Two brothers – Terry and Tommy Delaney were found guilty of manslaughter, but it was all spoiled for us because we couldn't even tell our pals that we had seen it all.

We did gather, from listening to conversations not meant for our sensitive ears, that the murdered boy had beaten up his wife when she had told him the expected wean wasn't his and her brothers had gone after him to teach him a lesson that went too far' as the Delaney's lawyer had said.

Mammy threw her coat out and Daddy gave her money for a new one.